The Paths of Evil

THE PATHS OF EVIL

Conspiracies, Plots, and Secret Societies

By Roberto de Mattei

Translated by Nicholas Reitzug

SOPHIA INSTITUTE PRESS
Manchester, New Hampshire

First published in Italian as *I sentieri del Male* © 2022 by Sugarco Edizioni S.r.l., Milan, Italy.

Cover by LUCAS Art & Design, Jenison, MI

Cover image: Crow (Pixabay 1894690); Reflection (Pixabay 83263); Embers (Pixabay 703651); Red and yellow abstract painting (Steve Johnson/Unsplash)

Sophia Institute Press
Box 5284, Manchester, NH 03108
1-800-888-9344
www.SophiaInstitute.com

Sophia Institute Press is a registered trademark of Sophia Institute.

paperback ISBN 978-1-64413-942-4

ebook ISBN 978-1-64413-943-1

Library of Congress Control Number: 2023949704

First printing

"It is impossible to love the good you do not know,
nor can you hate the evil
whose existence you do not even suspect."

"And so we went out to look once again upon the stars."

(*Inferno,* XXXIV, 139)

Contents

CHAPTER TWO
Conspiracies and Secret Societies

CHAPTER THREE
True and False Plots

The Paths of Evil

INTRODUCTION

Guide to Finding One's Way in the Tenebrous Labyrinth of Evil

Ever since the coronavirus intruded upon the world scene in January 2020, daily life for Western man has changed in an unexpected way. The desire to know the causes underlying events is ingrained in man's nature, and it comes as no surprise that these changes in our lives, as radical as they are confusing, have raised disturbing questions about the origin, the nature, and the consequences of the pandemic. This environment of concern and dismay has nourished the belief in a macro-plot organized by the secret forces that dominate history. The culture of suspicion, born in the French Revolution, has become the prevailing psychological attitude in a society of men who, no longer trusting in God, are wary of their neighbors. But it is precisely the practical atheism in which our society is immersed that inhibits many from comprehending that, in history, it is men, groups, and organized societies, secret as well as public, that act and place themselves in radical opposition to the natural and divine order; it is these that form the occult or "diabolic" dimension of history.

The following pages are meant to be a synthetic reconstruction of the plots and conspiracies, real or presumed, of the last five centuries. Above all, they propose to offer a guide, less informative than criteriological, to orientate us in this tenebrous labyrinth of evil.

Moral evil, which St. Paul defines as *mysterium iniquitatis* (2 Thess. 2:7), is a mystery terrible and profound. It has its roots in the freedom of the rational creature, called to unite itself with the divine will or to separate itself irremediably from it. The essence of this choice is moral: every man is called to direct his life toward the good or toward evil. And so, just as there exists a luminous genealogy of saints who ascend the ladder of the Highest Good, which is the Divine Being, so too there exists a dark genealogy of "ascetics of evil" who descend toward the abyss of nothingness.

A history of humanity that would ignore the existence of the heights of sanctity would be distorted, but a history that ignores the existence of the abyss of evil would likewise be deformed. Whoever fails to detest evil cannot love the good. And if one cannot love the good one does not know, then one cannot hate the evil whose existence one does not even suspect. This is the reason that has led me to shed some light on the "pathways of evil," after having dedicated a book to Divine Providence, the highest order of good.

CHAPTER ONE

Political Conspiracies and Crimes

1. Conspiracy Theories and Socio-Psychological Reductionism

Conspiracy theories have been the subject of a vast literary output that seeks to refute them by applying the principles of psychiatry and sociology.[1] These social sciences can certainly contribute to understanding historical events, because every human action has psychological roots and, to be understood, must be placed into its social context. But when psychological and sociological theories presume to offer the final explanation of reality, they fall into *reductionism*, one of the most widespread epistemological errors of our age. There is a philosophical principle, founded on common sense, according to which only that which is superior can explain what is inferior, and not vice versa.[2] The rewriting of history through sociology, psychology, statistics, and linguistics, transformed by "auxiliary sciences" into so-called primary sciences, undermines the credibility of these intellectual contributions.

According to some psychologists, conspiracy theories are a mental mechanism of self-defense born of a denial of reality, or of a mistrust of one's neighbor, with typically paranoic traits. From the

1 Cf. Joseph Uscinski, *Conspiracy Theories: A Primer*, Rowman & Littlefield, Lanham 2020, pp. 65–78.

2 Réginald Garrigou-Lagrange, *Introduzione allo studio di Dio* [*Introduction to the Study of God*], Fede e Cultura, Verona 2013, p. 59.

beginning of the twentieth century, the psychiatrists Paul Sérieux (1864–1947) and Joseph Capgras (1873–1950) listed among the forms of psychoses the so-called *délir d'interprétation*, which drives the subject to interpret every event of his life as proof of some scheming against him.[3] This is a clear-headed, reasoned madness consisting in the desire to attribute intentional causes to the smallest chance details, substituting objective reality with a subjective, arbitrary interpretation. The pathological error is not found in the factual materiality, but rather in its meaning.

The delirium of interpretation which Sérieux and Capgras apply to individual pathological cases is extended today to phenomena with a social nature. The historian Richard Hofstadter (1916–1970), in his *Paranoid Style in American Politics*, affirmed that the conspiratorial stance is a form of political paranoia that has characterized the history of the United States ever since the period of the American Revolution. The difference between the psychiatric paranoid and the social paranoid is in the fact that the former sees the entire world as conspiring against him, while the latter believes that the persecution meted out by occult powers is aimed against his political or religious group. But the political scientist Daniel Pipes, in his *Conspiracy: How the Paranoid Style Flourishes and Where It Comes From*, shows how an inability to live in the complex world of plotters and conspirators ensues when the guiding parameter becomes the "paranoid style."

Pipes allows for a distinction between conspiracies, which are real, and conspiracy theories, which exist only in the imagination, but he offers no objective criteria for distinguishing them, and the conclusion drawn from his pages is that even one who denounces true conspiracies is, in the final analysis, a paranoiac who falls into conspiratorial behavior and nourishes false conspiracy theories.

3 Paul Sérieux, Joseph Capgras, *Folies raisonnantes* [*Reasonable Follies*], Alcan, Paris 1909.

The problem is so intricate that according to the author of *Suspicious Minds*, the psychologist Rob Brotherton, conspiracy theories are born in the darkness of human minds, without representing a pathological deviation because everyone possesses "an innately suspicious mind."[4]

These analyses are limited by their vision of reality, a vision both relativistic and materialistic, in which our neurons are responsible for every intellectual choice, including conspiracy theories.[5] Not only God, but also human freedom is absent from this deterministic horizon.

2. Conspiracy Theories and Socio-Political Reductionism

The most nuanced critic of conspiracy theories remains Karl Popper (1902–1994). Beginning in the 1940s, the Austrian philosopher of science wrote in his *The Open Society and Its Enemies* that conspiracy theories circulating in society "derive from the erroneous theory that, whatever happens in society (especially events which people usually detest such as wars, unemployment, poverty, and famine) is the result of direct interventions of some powerful individuals and groups." This theory, according to Popper, would be "the typical result of the secularization of a religious superstition."[6] In his *Conjectures and Refutations*, Popper reiterates that "social conspiracy theories are a version of this theism, of the belief, that is, in a divinity whose tantrums and desires sustain all things. It is a consequence of the disappearance of any reference to God, and the subsequent question: 'Who stands in his place?'

4 Rob Brotherton, *Suspicious Minds: Why We Believe Conspiracy Theories*, Bloomsbury, London 2015, p. 19.

5 Michael Barkun moves on the socio-psychological level in his *Culture of Conspiracy: Apocalyptic Visions in Contemporary America*, University of California Press, Berkeley 2003, and Pierre-André Teguieff, in *L'Imaginaire du complot mondial: Aspects d'un mythe modern* [*The Global Conspiracy Fantasy: Aspects of a Modern Myth*], Mille Et Une Nuit, Paris 2006.

6 Karl Popper, *The Open Society and Its Enemies*, Routledge, London 1945.

This is now occupied by various powerful men and groups, sinister pressure groups whom one can impute for having organized the Great Depression and all other evils that afflict us."[7]

One can admit with Popper that a certain type of conspiracy theory secularizes the idea of Providence, but Popper believes neither in conspiracies nor in Divine Providence that guides history. His theories are based on the idea that truth does not exist and that the presumption of possessing truth is by nature totalitarian. For Popper, Communism and National Socialism have a common element: they presume to possess the absolute truth. The Austrian philosopher contrasts totalitarian societies with a model of democratic organization which he defines "open society," because it is contrary to every objective and universal affirmation. The concepts of good and evil, as well as those of true and false, in the Aristotelian sense of the words, are extraneous to his vision. Popper's sociology, like social psychology, is a reductionist theory that ignores the moral absolutes that are fundamental for those who hold a non-reductionist perspective.[8] The socio-psychological criticisms of conspiracy theories deprive themselves in this way of the rational possibility of demonstrating to be false whatever is under discussion. If nothing is absolutely true, nothing can be affirmed to be absolutely false.

Similarly reductionist is the vision of political scientists like Alessandro Campi, who only allow for the reality of "conspiracies" understood as "micro-plots" instigated by concrete historical subjects in view of a specific objective, while they negate the possibility of wide-scale conspiracies, which they define as "macro-conspiracies," existing

7 Karl Popper, *Conjectures and Refutations: The Growth of Scientific Knowledge*, Routledge, London 1962.

8 Cf. Carlos Cardona, *Metafisica del bene e del male* [*Metaphysics of Good and Evil*], Ares, Milan 1987; Ramon Garcia de Haro, *La vita cristiana* [*The Christian Life*] Ares, Milan 1995, pp. 336–37.

only in the mind of those who construct them.[9] The political horizon of Campi, as with his socio-psychological vision, gives attention only to one part of reality, excluding the possibility of a supra-political dimension of events.

The sociologist Massimo Introvigne, who dedicated many interesting books to the advent of the "New Age," while admitting the existence of "metaphysical conspiracies" of a "theological" or "esoteric" character that "elude the historian's empirical work,"[10] seems to limit himself in fact to an analysis devoid of criteria that might transcend the sociological dimension. It is necessary, therefore, that these contributions be integrated into a wider and more cogent vision of historical events.

3. The Philosophy of Christian History

Conspiracy theories are philosophies of history which cannot be understood in a purely psychological, political, or sociological perspective, reducing reality to the mere factual plane. Against postmodern historiographical relativism, it must be affirmed that the historian cannot proceed without having a philosophy of history and, in the case of a Catholic historian, a theology of history.

The historian researches the truth of the facts by means of rigorous verification, but also and above all the truth in interpreting events, which consists in understanding the causal relations that connect them, evaluating them in the light of principles that transcend the merely empirical dimension. If there are no principles that can

9 Alessandro Campi, "Congiura o complotto? Una distinzione analiticamente e storiograficamente necessaria" [*Congiure* and Plots? A Distinction Analytically and Historiographically Necessary], in *Congiure e complotti. Da Machiavelli a Beppe Grillo* [Congiure *and Plots: From Machiavelli to Beppe Grillo*], by A. Campi and Leonardo Varasano, Rubbettino, Soveria Mannelli 2016, pp. 21–36.

10 Massimo Introvigne, *Gli Illuminati e il Priorato di Sion* [*The Illuminati and the Priory of Sion*], Piemme, Casale Monferrato 2006, pp. 18–20.

judge historical facts from on high, everything that happens is, as such, a mere "value."

The perceptive philosopher of history Juan Donoso Cortés (1809–1853) wisely remarked that every political and social truth has as its foundation a theological truth, because theology is the science that embraces every social science.[11] According to Catholic theology, God creates, preserves, and directs all things to their appropriate end, but because He created man free, man too, with his will and his intelligence, contributes to the fulfillment of events, under the direction of Divine Providence which draws good out of evil and embraces the history of individuals as well as nations.[12]

Dom Prosper Guéranger (1805–1875) teaches, "History must be Christian if it is to be true; because Christianity is the complete truth; any historical system that prescinds from the supernatural order in the narration of facts is a false system that explains nothing and leaves the history of humanity in chaos and permanent contradiction."[13]

One who relativizes moral absolutes deprives himself of the necessary instruments for understanding how evil exists in history as a consequence of original sin, and that there are men who associate to commit evil in a systematic manner. The presence of criminal associations operating in secret, like the Mafia and many others, demonstrates this. It must be said that the Mafia is a criminal society not because it is secret, but because in secret it plans and carries out criminal actions. The associative secret as such is not evil: it becomes illicit only if the ends it seeks and the means it uses to attain them are

11 Juan Donoso Cortés, *Ensayo sobre el catolicismo, el liberalismo y el socialismo* [*Essay on Catholicism, Liberalism and Socialism*], in *Obras Completas*, Bac, Madrid 1970, p. 501.

12 St. Thomas Aquinas, *Summa theologiae*, q. 115, a. 6; q. 116, a. 1.

13 Dom Prosper Guéranger, *Le sens de l'histoire*, in *Essai sur le naturalisme contemporain* [*The Meaning of History*, in *Essay on Contemporary Naturalism*] Éditions Delacroix, 2004, p. 366.

illicit. Thus, secrets of state that concern internal or international security are legitimate, as is confidential information that public officials are held to keep secret as public servants. Every state has its secret services, today rebaptized "intelligence," to protect its own interests, within and beyond its border.

Furthermore, to the contrary of what one might imagine, Catholic associations have existed to do good in secret. One of these was, for example, the Confraternity of the Most Holy Sacrament, founded in Paris in 1630. This society gathered the most fervent souls in France at that time with the aim of "accomplishing all the good possible and removing all the evil possible, in every moment, in every place and for every person."[14] To this company belonged, among others, St. Vincent de Paul (1581–1660), St. John Eudes (1601–1680), and Fr. Charles de Condren (1588–1641), Superior General of the Congregation of the Oratorians. The deeds of saints help us to understand the deeds of the ascetics of evil.

Transparency is not necessarily a virtue and secrets are not always vices, although at times they may be a religious and moral obligation. The most inviolable secret is the absolute obligation imposed on the confessor to abstain from revealing what a penitent has said in the confessional to obtain sacramental absolution. The confessional secret is an obligation not only of ecclesiastical law but of divine law. Thus, the priest who violates this secret is excommunicated *latae sententiae*.[15]

4. *Congiure*, Conspiracies, and Plots

A conspiracy theory, according to socio-psychologists, is any conception of history that postulates the existence of enemies working in secret to strike their adversary. The hypothesis, for example, that the coronavirus

14 Cf. The entry of Msgr. Pietro Amato Frutaz, in *Enciclopedia cattolica*, vol. IV (1950), col. 79–80.

15 Canon 1388 of the current Code of Canon Law.

leaked in 2020 intentionally or incidentally from a Chinese bioweapons laboratory, is considered a "conspiracy theory" in the same way as the hypothesis that the pandemic was provoked by Western oligarchies to exterminate humanity. While the former hypothesis has been rendered probable by a great deal of evidence,[16] the latter is devoid of evidence that might support it. The socio-psychological criterion is not the reliability of the hypothesis, which ought to be considered true or fictional according to the evidence put forward in its support, but rather the subjective psychological attitude of those wanting to believe it true or false. In the socio-psychological perspective that disregards the concepts of good and evil, the only evil is to posit the existence of absolute truth, of "good guys" and "bad guys" that operate in history. In this relativistic perspective, one must admit that even the most absurd conspiracy theories carry out a positive role because, as Joseph Uscinski acknowledges, "the dichotomy true/false" cannot be used to criticize them.[17]

In fact, good and evil are not ontological but rather moral realities, present throughout history. The recognition of the existence of moral absolutes founded on "common sense" is the fundamental point of departure for the following pages.[18] But if the good is clear and coherent, evil is obscure and contorted. The reality of the world in which good and evil are interspersed like wheat and tares appears to us like a labyrinth at times. How should one think about these matters when confronting the difficult theme of secret societies and their plans in history?

16 Cf. Roberto de Mattei, *Le origini misteriose del coronavirus* [*The Mysterious Origins of the Coronavirus*], Edizioni Fiducia, Rome 2021.

17 J. Uscinski, "The Study of Conspiracy Theories," in *Argumenta*, 3,2 (2018), p. 237 (pp. 233–45).

18 R. Garrigou-Lagrange, *Le sens commun. La philosophie de l'être et les formules dogmatiques* [*Common Sense: The Philosophy of Being and Dogmatic Formulas*], Nouvelle Librairie Nationale, Paris 1926.

We shall propose a distinction that, like all schematizations, must not be taken as absolute, but only as an investigative itinerary: the distinction between *congiure*, conspiracy, and plot, terms that are often used as synonyms but, through their semantic and conceptual differences, can help us to understand better the hidden dimension of history.

The Italian word *congiura,* from the Latin term *coniurare,* is formed by *cum* (with) and *iurare* (to swear an oath), sharing an etymological origin with the German term *Verschwörung.* It indicates a secret pact, confirmed by a sworn oath, among a limited number of people, to eliminate an enemy.

The word *conspiracy* derives from the Latin *cum-spirare* (to breathe with, to be animated by the same spirit), and indicates a secret agreement to reach a certain objective which is broader in scope than *congiura.* Conspiracy can have a greater duration in time than a *congiura* and involves a greater number of participants. Its character is often political or ideological.[19]

The term *plot* indicates an intrigue or a secret plan and has modern and literary origins. The Latin etymologies of *congiura* and *conspiracy* help us understand the meaning of the terms, whereas for *plot,* it comes from *complot* which also means conspiracy although with the nuance of a storyline in development.[20] In the language of cinema and literature, the plot is the narrative development of a novel, a film, or a theatrical work. The word *plot* can be used as a synonym for *congiura* and *conspiracy,* but also in a sense that belongs more to fiction than to reality. However, *congiura,* conspiracy, and plot are not "comical pranks" that can be dismissed with a sarcastic

[19] Italian penal code establishes, for example, the crime of conspiracy in article 304 (*Cospirazione politica mediante accordo*) and 305 (*Cospirazione politica mediante associazione*).

[20] *The Oxford English Dictionary*, Oxford University Press, Oxford, vol. XI (1989), p. 1056.

tone, but rather pathways toward the abyss of evil that opposes God, an infinite abyss empty of all truth and good.

5. *Congiure* and Political Crimes

Congiure accompany history from its very beginning. We might not be sure that Catiline's was a true *congiura*, but we know that Junius Brutus and Cassius's was, namely the assassination of Julius Caesar, stabbed on March 15, 44 BC, in the famous Ides of March.[21] *Congiure* are generally enacted with the desire for vengeance for offenses suffered or with the intention of "overthrowing the tyrant" and "liberating the nation." In these there is no negation of the established social order. The *congiura* sees its success, generally speaking, in the assassination. The *congiura* par excellence was that of Brutus and Cassius, as well as that of the Sanhedrin against Jesus Christ, which succeeded thanks to Judas's betrayal. In the *Divine Comedy*, the last circle of the Inferno, portrayed in Canto XXXIV, is dominated by the figure of three-headed Lucifer, each of which adorned with the greatest traitors in history hanging from them, wracked for all eternity: Judas, Brutus, and Cassius. Judas is punished for his betrayal of Christ and the Church, while his two companions in punishment, mangled in the lateral mouths of Lucifer, are traitors against Caesar and therefore the empire.

In the Middle Ages, conspiracies or political assassinations were unknown with only rare exceptions. This can be explained by the specific character of medieval civilization, founded on the feudal pact, the relationship of reciprocal fidelity between vassal and lord.[22] In a society that gives supreme value to fidelity, betrayal is also one of

21 Paolo Mieli, *Il tribunale della storia. Processo alla falsificazione* [*The Tribunal of History: Falsification on Trial*], Rizzoli, Milan 2021, pp. 77–83.

22 Cf. François Ganshof, *Che cosa è il feudalismo* [*What Is Feudalism*], Einaudi, Turin 1997.

the worst crimes. Betrayal is a form of radical ingratitude, and no society cultivated gratitude like medieval society, which presupposes the recognition of a relationship of dependence between the giver and the receiver. Bertrand de Jouvenel observed, "What the medieval felt and expresses is that every man had a superior. This superior was his lord, his superior, his sovereign; who in his turn had a lord, a superior, a sovereign: thus, society offered in full view what Augustin Thierry magnificently called '*a great chain of obligations*.' "[23]

The historian Marcello Flores dedicated a book to the twentieth century titled *The Century of Betrayals,* but the greatest period of betrayal was that which closed the Middle Ages, an age of intrigues and conspiracies, when political assassinations were the inevitable outcome.[24] The most fertile period for conspiracies, therefore, was that of the Renaissance, when humanism was ascendant.[25]

George Minois, a French historian who dedicated a book to conspiracies and political assassinations in Europe, writes that "from the Carolingian Age until the thirteenth century, namely for more than five centuries, assassinations were relatively rare."[26] The situation

23 Bertrand de Jouvenel, *La sovranità* [*Sovereignty*], Giuffrè, Milan 1971 (1955), p. 214.

24 Marcello Flores, *Il secolo dei tradimenti* [*The Century of Betrayal*], il Mulino, Bologna 2017.

25 Renato Fubini, *L'Età delle congiure: i rapporti tra Firenze e Milano dal tempo di Piero a quello di Lorenzo de'Medici (1464-1478) [The Age of Conspiracies: Relations Between Florence and Milan from the Age of Piero to the Age of Lorenzo de'Medici (1464-1478)]*, in id., *Italia quattrocentesca. Politica e diplomazia nell'età di Lorenzo il Magnifico [Fourteenth Century Italy: Politics and Diplomacy in the Age of Lorenzo the Magnificent]*, Franco Angeli, Milan 1994. cf. also Francesca Russo, *Bruto a Firenze. Mito, immagine e personaggio tra Umanesimo e Rinascimento [Brutus in Florence: Myth, Image and Person Between Humanism and Renaissance]*, Editoriale Scientifica, Naples 2008.

26 George Minois, *Il pugnale e il veleno. L'assassinio politico in Europa (1400-1800)* [*The Dagger and the Poison: Political Assassination in Europe (1400-1800)*], Utet, Turin 2005, p. 5.

began to change when the Middle Ages declined and, from the fourteenth century onward, criminality enters into political practice. In 1345, Queen Joan of Naples strangled her husband Andrew, son of the King of Hungary; in 1382, Joan was in turn strangled at the behest of Charles of Durres, who became King of Naples and of Hungary, but was then assassinated as well four years later.

In Milan, conspiracies and crimes accompanied the rise of the Visconti dynasty. Stefano Visconti was assassinated in 1327; in 1355 his son Matteo II was assassinated by his brothers Galeazzo and Bernabò; in 1385, the same Bernabò, a libertine father of thirty-four children legitimate and illegitimate, was poisoned by his nephew Gian Galeazzo, first Duke of Milan; in 1404, Caterina Visconti, daughter of Bernabò and wife of Gian Galeazzo, was assassinated by order of her son Giovanni Maria Visconti, second Duke of Milan, who was also assassinated in 1412.

Sadly, Giovanni Maria Visconti was assassinated at the door of the Church of San Gottardo, just as Duke Galeazzo Maria Sforza was in the Church of Santo Stefano in Milan in 1476, while two years later Lorenzo and Giuliano de' Medici were assaulted in the Duomo of Florence at the moment of elevation. This demonstrates the lack of respect for the sacred in an age that affirmed the self-determination of the individual, increasingly indifferent to religious and moral law.

During humanism's ascendence in Italy, political assassination appears as just one instrument of conquest or consolidation of power, like marriage, war, or diplomacy. In the Rome of the pontiffs, the privileged means was poison, which best lent itself to dissemblance. According to the historian and bishop of Nocera Paolo Giovio (1483–1552), the Spanish Borgias, who included Pope Alexander VI (Rodrigo Borgia: 1431–1503) and his son Cesare Borgia (1475–1507), possessed a mysterious poison, "a powder of admirable whiteness, capable of fooling anyone, its flavor not altogether disagreeable,"[27] which eliminated its victims silently, among whom numbered at least three cardinals.

A professor at the University of Ferrara, Luca Zucchi, published an essay on "The Borgias and Toxicological Knowledge," in which he states that poison was a preparation made from arsenic and administered with other mineral substances that were coming into use around the end of the fourteenth century: silver nitrate, antimony, and lead acetate.[28] Nevertheless, the thesis made wildly popular by Msgr. Paolo Giovio and Francesco Guicciardini, which posits that Alexander VI had died because he mistakenly ingested poison he had prepared himself though it was destined for others, belongs to the "realm of fairytales," as Ludwig von Pastor observes.[29]

6. Anti-Papal Conspiracies

In the fifteenth century, classical literature inflamed minds, pushing some humanists to conspire to restore the ideas and customs of paganism. Stefano Porcari (1400–1453), a humanist who wanted to become a new Cola di Rienzo, conceived a plan of insurrection against Pope Niccolò V (1447–1455), with the aim of inaugurating in Rome a Republican form of government. The plan was to be carried out during the feast of the Epiphany of 1453. Porcari enlisted three hundred mercenaries to assault the Vatican, killing, if necessary, the pope and the cardinals, calling Romans to rebellion against the power of the pontiff and then proclaiming a republic of Rome. Baron von Pastor, who gives us a sweeping account of the conspiracy, writes that on the

27 Giovan Maria Bonelli, *Delle historie del suo tempo di mons. Paolo Giovio da Como [Several Histories of His Age by Msgr. Paolo Giovio da Como]*, Venice 1560, Book Two, p. 61.

28 *Lucrezia Borgia. Storia e mito* [*Lucrezia Borgia: History and Myth*], ed. by Michele Bordin and Paolo Trovato, Leo S. Olschki, Florence 2006, pp. 223–52.

29 Ludwig von Pastor, *Storia dei Papi dalla fine del Medio Evo* [*History of the Popes from the End of the Middle Ages*], Declée & Co., Rome 1942, vol. III, pp. 574–77.

sleeve of the formal outfit Porcari had designed for himself to wear when he became tribune, one could read stitched in gold, "Liberator of the City."[30] The conspiracy was discovered, however, and Porcari was arrested, tried, and hanged with several of his accomplices in Castel Sant'Angelo on January 9, 1453.

More insidious was the conspiracy discovered by the pontifical police in 1468. At the center of it was the Roman Academy, founded by the humanist Giulio Pomponio Leto (1428–1498). Illegitimate descendant of Count Giovanni Sanseverino, Pomponio Leto (his true name is still unknown) was a student of the humanist Lorenzo Valla (1407–1457) and held the chair of eloquence after him in Rome. A great admirer of Julian the Apostate,[31] Pomponio, according to the German historian Ferdinand Gregorovius (1821–1891), "completely undid himself in paganism. Like the ghost of an ancient man you could see him wandering among the Roman tombs and the sight of an ancient monument could move him to tears."[32] This neo-pagan humanist founded the Roman Academy with the aim of promoting ancient *romanità*, giving it "the forms of an ancient sacerdotal college or a classic Masonic lodge, whose pontifex maximus was the great Pomponio, while others later received inferior sacerdotal degrees."[33]

With the ancient pagan cults and an accent on Epicurean and materialist lifestyle, the Roman Academy cultivated the idea of deposing the papacy and substituting it with a reborn republic. In the last days of February 1468, the city of Rome discovered that the police had

30 Ibid., vol. I, pp. 574–75 and more extensively, pp. 565–86.

31 Stefano Trovato, *L'Imperatore Giuliano e Pomponio Leto: la prima decisa rivalutazione dell'Apostata* [*Emperor Julian and Pomponius Leto: The First Decisive Reassessment of the Apostate*], in *Atti dell'Istituto Veneto di Scienze, Lettere ed Arti. Classe di scienze morali, lettere ed arti*, CLXI (2002–2003), pp. 799–836.

32 Ferdinand Gregorovius, *Storia di Roma nel Medioevo* [*History of Rome in the Middle Ages*], Avanzini e Torraca Editori, Rome 1968, vol. VI, p. 345.

33 Ibid., p. 346.

carried out many arrests after having uncovered a conspiracy to assassinate Pope Paul II (1464–1471). The pope decreed the dissolution of the Roman Academy and informed the ambassadors to the Papal State of the conspiracy; the letters of some are still in our possession.[34] Pomponio Leto, who at that moment was detained in Venice awaiting trial on charges of sodomy, was extradited to Rome but, thanks also to the support he enjoyed, was cleared of the accusations of conspiracy and heresy, while Filippo Buonacorsi (1437–1496), the main defendant, succeeded in escaping, reaching Chios, where he was involved in a second conspiracy that sought to hand over the Greek island to the Ottomans. A study by Paola Medioli Masotti[35] evoked the hypothesis of an international political intrigue involving the Turkish sultan, intending to provoke a council against the pope or even a schism within the Church.

7. Conspiracies Against the Principe

In this period, poison was not the only means used to suppress political adversaries. The son of Alexander VI, Cesare Borgia, employed less discrete means, as happened in the assassination of his brother, Giovanni, in 1497. On June 14, the pope's lover, Vannozza Cattanei, held a party to celebrate the reconciliation of her two sons, Cesare, the twenty-two-year-old cardinal of Valencia, and Giovanni, the twenty-one-year-old Duke of Gandia. Returning from the celebration in the dark of night, Giovanni was attacked by Cesare's assassins and stabbed to death. His body was thrown into the Tiber, but the scene was noticed by a witness who informed the police. The cadaver was fished out and identified, but the guilty, though known by all, was not brought to justice.

[34] L. von Pastor, *Storia dei Papi* [*History of the Popes*], vol. II, pp. 313–15 and, more extensively, pp. 307–25.

[35] Paola Medioli Masotti, *L'Accademia romana e la congiura del 1468* [*The Roman Accademy and the* Congiura *of 1468*], in "Italia medioevale e umanistica", XXV (1982), pp. 189–204.

Two years later, Cesare Borgia assassinated Alfonso d'Aragona (1481–1500), Duke of Bisceglie, the second husband of his sister Lucrezia (1480–1519), she too the illegitimate daughter of the pope. The Duke of Bisceglie was assaulted on July 15, 1500, near his palace in Santa Maria del Portico, in Rome. He defended himself and was able to save himself. Cesare Borgia visited his wounded brother-in-law, murmuring maliciously in his ear that "what was not done at lunch, will be done at dinner." On August 18, Borgia burst into the room of the convalescing man with a gang of armed men and ordered one of them to strangle the sick man before his eyes. The justification Cesare gave his father was that Alfonso had plotted to kill him. Alexander VI approved of the crime and Lucrezia was given once more in marriage two years later to Duke Alfonso d'Este of Ferrara (1476–1534).

During the war in Romagna, the same Cesare Borgia discovered that some of his *condottieri* were plotting his harm. These characters were summoned to the castle of Magione in Umbria with the idea of organizing a coalition of princes against the Duke of Valentino. Cesare Borgia was informed and invited his enemies to a banquet in Senigallia, under the pretext of a definitive reconciliation. The conspirators fell into his trap and on December 31, 1502, were captured and murdered. Niccolò Machiavelli (1469–1527) dedicated a brief tract to this dramatic episode, the *Description of the Methods Adopted by the Duke Vallentino when Murdering Vitellozzo Vitelli, Oliverotto da Fermo, the Lord Paolo and the Duke of Gravina Orsini*, written in 1503.[36]

The episode was taken up by Machiavelli again in chapter seven of his most well-known work, *The Prince* (1513), in which he proposes

[36] Niccolò Machiavelli, *Descrizione del modo tenuto dal Duca Valentino nello ammazzare Vitellozzo Vitelli, Oliverotto da Fermo, il Signor Paolo e il duca di Gravina Orsini in Senigaglia* [*Description of the Methods Adopted by the Duke Vallentino when Murdering Vitellozzo Vitelli, Oliverotto da Fermo, the Lord Paolo and the Duke of Gravina Orsini*], in *Opere politiche*, Le Monnier, Florence 1969, pp. 643–54.

the figure of Cesare Borgia as a model of the new Renaissance prince. Machiavelli's judgment was not moral, but political, in an epoch in which politics had been emancipated from morality and had absorbed it. In the *Florentine Histories* (1520–1525), Machiavelli proposes a bare but efficacious description of the conspiracies of his time, whose protagonists are real men, described with their ambitions and passions: Piero de' Bardi who conspired against the oligarchs of the city of Florence (1340); Battista Canneschi against Annibale Bentivoglio (1445); Stefano Porcari against Pope Niccolò V (1453); Francesco Neroni against Piero de' Medici (1466); Bernardo Nardi against the chief magistrate of Florence Cesare Petrucci (1470).[37] The last and most important conspiracy was the failed attempt (as were many of the others) of the de' Pazzi family against that of the Medici (1478). The conspiracy led to the murder of Giuliano and the wounding of Lorenzo the Magnificent, without however bringing to an end Medici power over Florence, as they had planned.[38]

Also, in the *Discourses on Livy* (1513–1519), Machiavelli treats in a systematic way the theme of conspiracies, to which he dedicated an entire chapter, enriched with historical examples. In this chapter, the sixth of Book III,[39] he goes beyond a mere historical review of conspiracies, proposing to draw them into a new political category.[40] He traves them throughout history, beginning with the time of the

[37] N. Machiavelli, *Le istorie fiorentine* [*Florentine Histories*], Le Monnier, Florence 1990.

[38] Elena Fasano Guarini, *Congiure "contro alla patria" e congiure "contro ad uno principe" nell'opera di Niccolò Machiavelli* [*Conspiracies "Against the Country" and Conspiracies "Against a Prince" in the Work of Niccolò Machiavelli*], in *Complots et conjurations dans l'Europe moderne*, École Française de Rome, Rome 1996, pp. 9–53.

[39] N. Machiavelli, *Discorsi sopra la prima Deca di Tito Livio* [*Discourses on Livy*], Book VI, in *Opere politiche*, cit., pp. 511–37.

[40] A. Campi, *Machiavelli e le congiure* [*Machiavelli and the* Congiure], in N. Machiavelli, *Sulle congiure* [*On* Congiure], Rubbettino, Soveria Mannelli 2014, p. 11.

Duke of Athens, passing through the late fifteenth-century conspiracies (against the Medici, the Sforza, and the Aragona, as outlined above) down to the events which Machiavelli lived through, such as the conspiracy of the Pazzi, the conspiracy of the Magione (1502), the plot against Alfonso d'Este (1506), the plot against Giuliano de' Medici (1513), and that against Pandolfo Petrucci in Sienna (1508).

Machiavelli is against conspiracies because what concerns him most is the stability of power, while conspiracies are generally sources of instability and social disorder. "Because the ability to wage open war against a prince is conceded to few: the ability to conspire against him is conceded to each. On the other hand, private men enter into no undertaking more dangerous or reckless than this one; because this is difficult and dangerous in every one of its aspects. Whence it is that many attempt this, and so few attain the desired end. For this reason, therefore, princes should learn to abstain from this danger, private men should timidly consider the idea; no, let them learn to be content to live under that rule that fate meted out to them; I shall speak of it diffusely, leaving out no notable case attesting to one or the other. And truly, that sentence of Cornelius Tacitus is golden which says: that men have to honor the things of the past and to obey those present; and ought to desire good principles, and, however it is they are made, to tolerate them. And truly he who acts otherwise, more often than not, ruins himself and his nation."[41]

8. The Conspiracies of the Rosicrucians

Conspiracies and political crimes are not only an Italian prerogative. In England in 1471, during the war between the Lancasters and the Yorks, Duke Edward of York had King Henry VI assassinated. Edward ascended to the throne with the name of Edward IV. In 1483, his son

[41] N. Machiavelli, *Delle congiure* [*On* Congiure], in *Discorsi sopra la prima Deca di Tito Livio* [*Discourses on Livy*], p. 511.

Edward V was in turn imprisoned and secretly killed by his uncle, the Duke of Gloucester, who took the name Richard III. But he died two years later fighting in the Battle of Bosworth, which brought about the end of the War of the Roses and the ascendency to the throne of the Tudor dynasty.

The works of William Shakespeare (1564–1616) immortalized many conspiracies, from *Richard III* to *Macbeth,* from *Othello* to *Hamlet.* Conspirators and political assassins in this period enjoyed a good reputation. Humanists, in their admiration for antiquity, preferred Brutus the tyrannicide to Caesar the tyrant. In *Julius Caesar,* Shakespeare makes Brutus into a historical hero who combats tyranny, although he is not innocent of the fault of treason, expressed in the last words Caesar says to Brutus, "*Tu quoque, Brute, fili mi*!" (You too, Brutus, my son!). These words, derived from Suetonius, entered into history to express the coincidence of crime, betrayal, and maximum ingratitude.[42]

The epoch in which Shakespeare wrote was also that in which the existence of secret societies of an esoteric character emerged, such as that of the Rosicrucians, spoken of at the beginning of the seventeenth century when two anonymous manifestos were published in Germany, the *Fama Fraternitatis* (1614) and the *Confessio Fraternitatis* (1615), and in relation to these, the *Chemical Nuptials* (*Chymische Hochzeit*) of the Lutheran theologian Johan Valentin Andreae (1586–1654). The existence of Christian Rosenkreutz, founder of the confraternity, is probably legendary, although many scholars are convinced that the Rosicrucians really existed and that their aim was the destruction of Catholic Rome. This thesis is sustained, for example, by the historian of secret societies Jean Marquès-Rivière (1903–2000), highlighting the kinship of the

42 Tranquillo G. Suetonius, *De vita Caesarum,* Liber I, *Divus Iulius,* LXXXII.

Rosicrucians with Cathar esotericism on one side and with radical Protestantism on the other.[43]

The philosopher of history Frances A. Yates (1899–1981), in two important books dedicated to *The Rosicrucian Enlightenment* (1972) and *The Occult Philosophy in the Elizabethan Age*, lifted a veil from this page, affirming that the writings of the Rosicrucians were part of a propaganda campaign orchestrated to support the project of the conversion of Europe to Protestantism, led by the Calvinist Prince Friedrich V of the Palatinate (1596-1632). The enemies were the House of Austria and the Jesuits, who in the sixteenth and seventeenth centuries constituted the backbone of the Catholic Counter Reform movement. "For the Rosicrucian, the Hapsburg-Jesuit alliance simply represented the Antichrist" and the imaginary Order of the Rosicrucian was devised as "a specular image of the Jesuit Order."[44]

Yates dedicated a book to Giordano Bruno and the Hermetic tradition, in which she inserts the "Bruno case" into the history of conspiracies and esotericism. The Renaissance was defined by the philosopher Paolo Rossi as "the time of magicians," and Giordano Bruno (1448–1600) was a "magician" searching for extraordinary powers to dominate nature, removing it from God's governance.[45] Besides Bruno's magical arts, one remembers his spy activity, carried out under the pseudonym of Henri Fagot over the course of the two years and more that he spent in London in the home of the French ambassador Michel de Castelnau.

According to the historian John Bossi, Bruno was at the service of Francis Walsingham (1534–1590), the ferocious head of secret

[43] Jean Marquès-Rivière, *Histoire des doctrines esotériques* [*A History of Esoteric Doctrines*], Payot, Paris 1970, pp. 337–54.

[44] Frances A. Yates, *The Rosicrucian Enlightenment*, Routledge & Kegan, London 1972, p. 271.

[45] Paolo Rossi, *Il tempo dei maghi. Rinascimento e modernità* [*The Age of Magicians: Renaissance and Modernity*], Raffaello Cortina, Milan 2006.

services under Elizabeth I.[46] The French ambassador, like Giordano Bruno, was Catholic, while Walsingham had received the task from the English queen of uncovering and suppressing the conspiracies of Catholics. Bruno was therefore not only an apostate of the Catholic Faith, but a despicable informant who revealed information that sent many Catholics to prison and certain death.

The history of the Rosicrucians concerns more than just conspiracies; it also has to do with the occult which developed in Europe from alchemy, from magic and from Jewish Kabbalah. The Protestant theologian Philipp Melanchthon (1497–1560), friend and counselor to Luther and nephew of Johannes Reuchlin (1455–1522), who initiated him into the study of the Kabbalah and divinization, was convinced that in the fifteenth century, after the fall of Constantinople to the Turks, the learned of Byzantium had brought to Florence the Hermetic tradition of the Egyptians and Greeks.

The reference is to the Council of Florence of 1439, when numerous Byzantine philosophers and theologians arrived in Italy in the train of Emperor John VIII Palaiologos. One of these scholars was Gemistos Plethon (1392–1448) who considered himself the depository of a *prisca theologia*, which included forms of magic and astral worship.[47] The Florentines were not content to furnish these exiles with hospitality, but realizing the importance of their notions, they honored them, offering them means of sustenance and study.

Some humanists, such as Marsilio Ficino (1433–1499) and Giovanni Pico della Mirandola (1463–1494), took up the syncretic theses. Thus, the Hermetic sciences flourished once more in the

46 John Bossi, *Giordano Bruno and the Embassy Affair*, Yale University Press, New Haven 1991.

47 Cesare Vasoli, *"Prisca theologia" e scienze occulte nell'umanesimo fiorentino*, in *Storia d'Italia* [*"Prisca Theology" and the Occult Sciences in Florentine Humanism*], Annali, 25, *Esoterismo*, ed. by Gian Mario Cazzaniga, Einaudi, Turin 2010, p. 183.

city of the Medici and, according to Melanchthon, the center of Lutheranism, Wittenberg, had the task of continuing Florence's cult of arcane wisdom.[48]

According to Frances Yates, the Rosicrucian manifestos published in Germany were the result of a "continental mission" accomplished in Bohemia by John Dee (1527–1608), cabalist and astrologer of Queen Elizabeth.[49] Dee, who specialized in conjuring spirits through crystal spheres, reached Bohemia in 1585, together with his alchemist colleague Edward Kelley (1555–1597), who claimed he communicated with the angels by means of the "Enochian language." Kelley had convinced Dee that by order of the "angels" they were to share all things in common, including their wives. The two magicians were received with full honors by Emperor Rudoph II (1552–1612), an enthusiast of the occult, in his royal castle in Hradčany, Prague.

In April of 1588, another unique personality arrived in Prague, Abramo Colorni (1544–1599), whose feats were narrated in detail by the historians Ariel Toaff and Daniel Jütte.[50] Colorni, born of a Jewish family from Mantua, was not only an alchemist and cabalist, but also an inventor of bombs of every sort, like the repeating harquebus, and was known for "being able to escape any cell, or any closed space, whatever the structure of the chains which impaired him."[51] Colorni stayed nine years in Prague where, as Toaff writes, "the confused occupations of the alchemist, the flashes and smoke of his metallurgical transformations, the boiling of liquids in the alembic stills and retorts,

48 Delio Cantimori, *Umanesimo e religione nel Rinascimento* [*Humanism and Religion in the Renaissance*], Einaudi, Turin 1975, pp. 266–67.

49 F. A. Yates, *The Rosicrucian Enlightenment*, pp. 36–38; *Cabala e occultismo nell'età elisabettiana* [*The Occult Philosophy in the Elizabethan Age*], Kegan Paul, London 1979, pp. 127–39.

50 Daniel Jütte, *The Age of Secrecy: Jews, Christians, and the Economy of Secrets, 1400–1800*, Yale University Press, New Haven 2015, pp. 116–23.

51 Carlo Colombero, *Colorni Abramo*, in *Dizionario Biografico degli Italiani*, vol. 27 (1982), p. 467 (pp. 466–68).

the suffocated voices of spirits and necromancers all rose with the other noises of the city into the din of the alleyways of the *Judenstadt* (the ghetto) and their sound was understood perfectly."[52]

These seekers of the philosophers' stone ended in a bad way. After returning to England in 1589, Dee died in misery at Mortlake on March 26, 1608. Kelley fell into disgrace, was imprisoned, and died on November 1, 1597, in Prague, after having broken his leg in an attempt to escape from prison. Colorni returned to Mantua where he died, perhaps of poisoning, toward the end of 1599.

If it is true that the Rosicrucian manifestos date to Dee's "mission" in Bohemia, what the magicians planned in their alembic stills was the destruction of the empire of Rudolph II, the sovereign who was hosting them. Rudolph fell prey to hallucinations and spells of depression, only to end his life imprisoned in the royal castle of his brother Matthias II who reigned in Austria and Bohemia until 1619.[53] Then, after the ascension of Ferdinand II Hapsburg (1578–1637), the Battle of White Mountain on November 8, 1620, near Prague, marked the victory of the Catholic Counter-Reformation and the House of Austria, definitively scuttling the political projects of the Protestants and the Rosicrucians.

In Italy, Francesco Giuseppe Borri (1627–1695) was considered to have close ties with the Rosicrucians. He was an extravagant alchemist and healer, who believed he was the *Prochristus*, invested with the mission of healing corrupt Christianity. Condemned by the Inquisition in 1660 for heresy, he wandered throughout Europe, from Strasbourg to Copenhagen, until he was arrested in Turkey and extradited to Rome, where in 1672 he was condemned to life in prison, serving his time in Castel Sant'Angelo.

[52] Ariel Toaff, *Il prestigiatore di Dio. Avventure e miracoli di un alchimista ebreo nelle corti del Rinascimento* [*God's Conjurer: Adventures and Miracles of a Jewish Alchemist in Renaissance Courts*], Rizzoli, Milan 2010, p. 154.

[53] F. A. Yates, *The Occult Philosophy in the Elizabethan Age*, pp.110–13.

A Rosicrucian network was organized by another enigmatic personality, Federico Gualdi, who appeared in the Republic of Venice in the mid-1600s only to disappear around 1680 after having organized the sect of the "Knights of the Aurea and Rosicrucian."[54] According to one of his biographies, doctors, literary types, and nobles belonged to this sect, "united by a heterodox vision of faith and by their attraction to esotericism and to scientific debate."[55]

Among them there were figures tied to the Roman court of Queen Christina of Sweden (1626–1689), such as the Marquis Francesco Maria Santinelli (1627–1697) and the Marquis Massimiliano Savelli Palombara (1614–1685), who dedicated himself to alchemy, the fusion of metals, and the study of medicinal herbs in his villa in Rome, in which a "magical door" is still visible.

According to legend, Federico Gualdi, who possessed an "elixir of long life," encountered Giacomo Casanova (1725–1798) in the 1770s and stayed in St. Petersburg toward the end of the century. Like him, the Count of Saint-Germain (1712–1784) was an alchemist and adventurer, and was the object of much talk claiming he had discovered the elixir of youth, thanks to which he claimed to have been living already for centuries. These fantasies attracted weak minds toward the occult disciplines, from which they were freed only with great difficulty. Rationalism and magical irrationalism developed in parallel in the years of the "crisis of the European conscience," of which the French historian Paul Hazard (1878–1944) wrote.[56]

54 Federico Barbierato, *Rosacroce, libertini e alchimisti nella società veneta del secondo Seicento: i Cavalieri dell'Aurea e Rosa Croce* [*Rosicrucians, Libertines, and Alchemists in Venetian Society in the Second Half of the Seventeenth Century: The Knights of the Aurea and Rosa Croce*], in *Storia d'Italia*, Annals, 25, *Esoterismo*, pp. 323–57.

55 Ibid., p. 333.

56 Paul Hazard, *La crise de la conscience européenne (1680–1715)* [*The Crisis of European Conscience (1680–1715)*], Boivin, Paris 1935.

9. Occult Sciences and Poisonings

The search for the "elixir of long life" is specular to the search for poisonous substances that can lead more efficiently to death. Both searches are often practiced by the same environments steeped in sorcery. Between the sixteenth and the seventeenth centuries, the art of poisoning became a science, perfected by Giulia Tofana, a court lady from Palermo, who around 1640 invented "Tofana water." Taking its name from the inventor, it was a colorless, odorless, flavorless poison, capable of provoking an apparently natural death in the span of a few days. After having admitted to selling enough poison to kill six hundred people between 1633 and 1651, on July 5, 1659, Giulia Tofana was condemned and executed in Campo de' Fiori in the heart of Rome, along with her daughter (or sister) Girolama Spera and three other women guilty of having poisoned their husbands.

Just a few years later, in 1672, in Paris, when the cavalry officer Godin de Sainte-Croix died, several of his letters were found in which he accused his lover Marie-Madeleine d'Aubray (1630–1676), the Marquis of Brinvilliers, of having poisoned her father, her two brothers and her sister with "Tofana water" to seize their part of the inheritance. The Marquis of Brinvilliers was put on trial and executed in 1676.

The investigation following the detailed inquiry conducted by an honest magistrate, Gabriel-Nicolas de La Reynie (1625–1709), extended throughout the Parisian neighborhood of Saint-Denis where there was a high concentration of astrologers, fortune-tellers, and witch doctors. Louis XIV gave extraordinary powers to an investigative commission called the *Commission de l'Arsénal* and the so-called "Poison Affair" opened in Paris, a trial that involved even the tight circle of the sovereigns and led to the arrest of about three hundred people involved in the illegal sale of poison, in the homicide of newborns, and in the traffic of consecrated hosts.

At the center of these crimes was the haberdasher Catherine Deshayes, known as La Voisin (1640–1680) from the surname of her husband. Madame La Voisin had set up a satanic chapel in which priests such as the Abbot Etienne Guibourg (1610–1686) celebrated horrible blasphemous rites, culminating in the sacrificial offering to demons of children with their throats slit or aborted fetuses. The Marquis Françoise-Athénaïs de Montespan (1640–1707), the King's favorite, participated in some of the ceremonies. She was obliged to leave the court and retire to a convent, while Catherine La Voisin was condemned to death with thirty-five others. Madame La Voisin violently denied receiving the confessor and the crucifix and died blaspheming at the stake,[57] while Marie-Madeleine d'Aubray, before being decapitated, repented and confessed in the hands of the Abbé Edme Poirot (1631–1713).[58]

The popes had already intervened with numerous bulls to encourage the inquisitors and suppress the occult sciences, from Innocent VIII (*Summi desiderantes* of December 6, 1484) and Alexander VI (*Cum acceperimus* of 1494) to Paul V (*Omnipotentis Dei* of March 20, 1623), but the so-called "Black Mass," which traces back to the satanism of the early centuries, was described for the first time in great detail in the acts of the La Voisin trial, which opens an impressive glimpse into the corruption at the court of Louis XIV.[59] As during the age of humanism in Italy, the *Grand*

[57] *Recueil des lettres de Madame la Marquise de Sevigné à Madame la comtesse de Grignan sa fille* [*Collection of letters from Madame la Marquise de Sevigné to her daughter Madame la Comtesse de Grignan*], Jean-Edme Dufour & Phil. Roux Imprimeurs, vol. V, Maestricht 1730, letter of February 23, 1680, p. 260.

[58] G. Roullier, *La marquise de Brinvilliers. Récit de ses derniers moments. Manuscript du P. Pirot, son confesseur* [*The Marquise de Brinvilliers. Account of her last moments. Manuscript by P. Pirot, her confessor*], 2 vol., A. Lamerre, Paris 1883.

[59] The original documents are found in the *Archives de la Bastille. Documents inédits,* collected and published by François Ravaisson-Mollien (19 vol.), A. Durand et Pedone-Lauriel, Paris 1866–1904, in volumes VI (1873) and VII (1874).

Siècle of the Sun King was an epoch of artistic magnificence, but of profound moral depravity.

10. From the Wars of Religion to Tyrannicide

After the Protestant conspiracy of Amboise in France, hatched in 1560 by the Huguenots to bring to power the Prince of Condé, the most celebrated conspiracy was certainly the St. Bartholemew's Day Massacre, on August 24, 1572, in Paris, during the Wars of Religion. Responsible for the slaughter was Catherine de' Medici (1519–1589), the only direct and legitimate descendant of Lorenzo the Magnificent, who incarnated in her person all the ambiguity of the Medici dynasty. Her true talent, according to the historian Jean Orieux, was her ability to utilize plots and intrigues of every type to attain her ends.[60] Catherine had Machiavelli's *The Prince* in her blood, but she had also suffered from early childhood the fascination of the occult sciences: she could not live far from her astrologers Cosimo Ruggieri (d. 1615) and the famous Nostradamus (Michel de Nostredame; 1503–1566), and she availed herself of the services of her "Maestro perfumer" Renato Bianco, known as René Florentin (d. 1568), an alchemist and the court poisoner.[61]

Catherine de' Medici, mother of three sovereigns of France (Francis II, Charles IX, and Henry III), succeeded in convincing her son Charles IX of the existence of a plot against the royal family and in obtaining full power for a preemptive action against the Huguenots who were gathered in Paris on the occasion of the marriage of Henry of Navarre and Margherita of Valois. On the night between

[60] Jean Orieux, *Un'italiana sul trono di Francia* [*An Italian on the Throne in France*], tr. It. Mondadori, Milan 2018, p. 286.

[61] Eugène Defrance, *Catherine de Médicis, ses astrologues et ses magiciens envoûteurs. Documents inédits sur la diplomatie et les sciences occultes du XVIe siècle* [*Catherine de Medici, Her Astrologers and Bewitching Magicians. Unpublished Documents on Sixteenth-Century Diplomacy and Occult Sciences*], Mercure de France, Paris 1911.

August 23 and 24, 1572, several thousand Huguenots were massacred in Paris and in the provinces. As a consequence of the carnage, the religious conflict was embittered, and in the successive years Henry of Guise (1550–1588), leader of the Catholic league, was betrayed and assassinated by Henry III (1551–1589). The King invited the Duke of Guise to the castle of Blois where he had his personal guard, the so-called "*quarante-cinq*," waiting in arms. The Duke was warned of the danger, but he did not hesitate to proceed to the royal castle where, on December 23, 1588, he was assassinated, despite mounting a tenacious resistance, wounding several of his aggressors. To prevent his remains from being treated as a martyr of the Catholic party, his body was burned and the ashes thrown into the Loire. The same day, her son Charles and brother Louis Cardinal of Lorraine were arrested and killed, while a third brother escaped death miraculously. In 1908, one of the first silent films was created in France based on this episode, titled *L'Assassinat du duc de Guise*.

Historical vindication often comes to conspirators whom we see dying the same violent death as their victims. On August 1, 1589, Henry III was killed in the royal castle of Saint-Cloud, stabbed with a poisoned dagger to the abdomen by a young third order Dominican, Jacques Clément (1567–1589), wanting to vindicate the Duke of Guise.[62] The death of Henry III marked the end of the Valois dynasty, to which the House of Bourbon succeeded. But the first sovereign of this dynasty as well, Henry IV, was assassinated on May 14, 1610, by François Ravaillac. The theory of a Catholic conspiracy was designed around this regicide, based on the book *De rege et regis institutione* (1598) by the Spanish Jesuit Juan de Mariana (1563–1624). On July 6, 1610, the general of the Jesuits, Claudio Acquaviva, in order to banish every suspicion, published a decree in which he proclaimed, "With

[62] Pierre Chevallier, *Les Régicides: Clément, Ravaillac, Damiens* [*The Regicides: Clement, Ravaillac, Damiens*], Fayard, Paris 1989.

the present decree, we order in virtue of sacred obedience and under pain of excommunication and other punishments reserved to our judgment, that no religious of our Society should take the liberty to affirm, publicly or in private, neither in his teachings nor in the counsels he gives, and even less in his written works, that a person might have the right, under whatsoever pretext, to kill kings or princes, or to plot their death."[63] Despite this unequivocal position, the Jesuits continued to be accused of conspiring against sovereigns.

11. Conspiracies and Tyrannicide

The age of conspiracies, between 1400 and 1800, coincides with that of political assassinations, integrated into European culture under the name of tyrannicide, as Minois has well explained.[64]

The term *tyrant* indicates the illegitimate origin of the use of power. St. Thomas Aquinas, in his *Summa Theologiae*,[65] and in *De Regimine principum*,[66] is the author of the first reflection on the problem of the liceity or lack thereof as regards the killing of a tyrant. According to the Angelic Doctor, the tyrant cannot be killed by private initiative if he abuses his governance. However, if it is necessary for the common good and there exists no higher authority to which one can appeal, the entire nation is permitted to rise up against him.

In the late fifteenth and early sixteenth centuries, these Thomistic lines of thought were taken up again by such doctors as St. Robert Bellarmine (1542–1621) and Francisco Suarez (1548–1617).[67] Protestants accused them of being "Monarchomachs," utilizing a term

63 Georges Minois, *Il pugnale e il veleno* [*The Dagger and the Poison*], cit., p. 93.

64 Ibid., p. 354.

65 St. Thomas Aquinas, *Summa theologiae*, I-II, q. 105, a. 1, ad. 2.

66 Aquinas, *De Regimine principum*, I, 6.

67 Carlo Giacon, S. J., *La seconda scolastica*, vol. III. *I problemi giuridico-politici. Suarez, Bellarmino, Mariana* [*The Second Scolastic, vol. III: The Juridical-Political Problems: Suarez, Bellarmine, Mariana*], Fratelli Bocca, Milan 1950.

introduced by the Scottish jurist William Barclay (1546–1608) in the treatise *De regno et regali potestate* (1600), indicating the political writers who support the right of the people to overthrow and even kill monarchs guilty of oppressing the religious life of their subjects. St. Robert Bellarmine replied with his *Tractatus de Potestate Summi Pontificis* (1610) in which he clarified with precision Catholic doctrine on this complex theme.[68]

St. Pius V, pope from 1566 to 1572, was accused of having encouraged the so-called Ridolfi Plot against Queen Elizabeth (1533–1612), who ascended to the English throne after having imprisoned her rival Mary Stuart. The Florentine banker Roberto Ridolfi (1531–1612), who lived in London, was her trusted man in England.[69] The pope entrusted to him the mission of working secretly for the restoration of the Catholic Church in England, assuring him a congruous financial support. Ridolfi established contacts with several English Catholic noblemen who rose up in arms against the usurper. The rebellion failed and was repressed in blood due to the lack of support from King Phillip II of Spain. On February 25, 1570, St. Pius V promulgated the papal bull *Regnans in excelsis,* by which he excommunicated Queen Elizabeth I, declaring her forfeit of her presumed right to the English crown.[70] The Dominican pope had not sinned by imprudence, but rather had taken inspiration from the teaching of his confrère Thomas Aquinas, who authorized the possibility of rebellion against the principe, under the condition that the common good required it and that there was a serious and concrete possibility of success.

68 St. Robert Bellarmine, *Tractatus de Potestate Summi Pontificis adversus Gulielmum Barclaium,* in *Opera,* B. Gualtheri, Coloniae Agrippinae 1617, pp. 829–995.

69 Cf. R. de Mattei, *Pio V. Storia di un Papa santo* [*Pius V: The History of a Saintly Pope*], Lindau, Turin 2021, pp. 210–14.

70 *Bullarium Romanum,* Dalmezzo, Augustae Taurinorum 1860, vol. VII, pp. 810 ff.

The so-called Gunpowder Plot, which the English called the Jesuit Treason, was ill-advised in its means and objectives. It was hatched between 1604 and 1605 to kill James I (1586–1625) and the lords meeting in Parliament by means of the explosion of a large quantity of gunpowder during the opening of the assembly. The conspiracy was discovered and was attributed to the Jesuits, who had not actually taken part in it. Over the course of the anti-Catholic persecutions that followed, Fr. Thomas Garnet, S.J. (1575–1608) was drawn and quartered in Tyburn on June 23, 1608, and is listed among the holy English martyrs today. The Gunpowder Plot offered the pretext for establishing unjust laws against English Catholics. Whoever did not contract marriage before a Protestant pastor, whoever refused Protestant baptism for their children, whoever refused to bury their dead in a Protestant cemetery, whoever refused to attend the divine services of the Anglicans had to pay heavy fines and risked incarceration.[71]

In France and England, regicide (attempted or achieved) was punished by drawing and quartering. In this way François Ravaillac (1578–1610), the assassin of Henry IV, and Robert-François Damiens (1715–1757), a lunatic who attempted to assassinate King Louis XV, were killed. Damiens's abdomen was cut open, and boiling oil and burning resin were poured into the wound. The operation was repeated for his limbs as well. The legs and arms of the condemned were then bound to four horses that were set off in opposite directions. But the limbs of the condemned did not cede and the horrible torture lasted for hours, as described in detail by the executioner Sanson.[72]

71 L. von Pastor, *Storia dei Papi* [*History of the Popes*], cit., vol. XII, pp. 440–41.

72 Clément Henri Sanson, *Le memorie dei carnefici di Parigi* [*Memories of the Slaughter of Paris*], tr. It. Messaggerie Pontremolesi, Milan 1989, pp. 157–65.

Neither Ravaillac nor Damiens challenged the French monarchy. They wanted to strike the person, not the principle. Aversion toward divine right monarchy was born in Enlightenment environments in which the regicides were mentioned as heroes.

Voltaire published the posthumous testament of Jean Meslier (1664–1729), a secretly apostate priest, who died from suicide. Meslier wished that all the great and noble of the earth "were hung and strangled with the guts of the last priest" and launched an appeal to the regicides of all times: "Where are the generous defenders of the public freedom that chased the kings and tyrants from their countries? Where are the Jacques Cléments? And the Ravaillac of our France? Are there any left in our century? And in any century? To kill and stab all of these detestable monsters and enemies of humankind?"[73]

12. The Conspiracy Against the Jesuits

In the mid–1700s, the Jesuits reached the height of their power with 22,500 religious in 39 provinces and 1,563 foundations. They were confessors and counsellors to sovereigns, and they educated youth in their universities and colleges, but above all they were the most intransigent defenders of the pope and the most dogged adversaries of all the heretical currents, and constituted the main bulwark of Catholic social order.

In this age, the so-called "*parti philosophique*" organized a systematic attack on the Christian foundations of society. Voltaire (1694–1778) was the head of this party, which proposed "exterminating the infamy," the Church, that is, and Catholic religion. The formula *Écrasez l'infâme* is often abbreviated by Voltaire with the initials "*Écrlinf,*" as in his letter to Étienne Noël Damilaville

[73] *Œuvres de Jean Meslier*, Anthropos, Paris 1970, vol. III, pp. 132–36.

(1723–1768) of July 26, 1762.[74] It concluded thus: "I end all my letters saying, *Écr. l'inf.*,... as Cato always said: *This is my opinion, that Carthage be destroyed.*"[75]

Voltaire's correspondence, some thousand letters written to the philosopher-king Friedrich II of Prussia (1712–1786), to d'Alembert (1717–1783), and to other personalities of the Enlightenment, offers us more than a project, a spirit. Voltaire wrote to d'Alembert on July 24, 1760: "Would it be possible that five or six men of merit who come to an agreement should not succeed, following the example we have of twelve boors [that would be the Apostles], not to be able to? It seems to me the success in this matter is an infinite honor."[76] On February 25, 1758, he had written to d'Alembert that the plan would be carried out within twenty years, but twenty years later, in 1778, Voltaire died without having witnessed the fulfillment of the endeavor.[77] Six weeks before his death, on April 15, 1778, Friedrich II wrote the philosopher a letter in which he registered his failure: "Your plan was to sink the infamy ... but the foundations remain, the weakness and the credulity of the human mind always prevail over reason and over the truth that the philosophers teach. Man is made for error."[78]

Part of Voltaire's project came to fruition, however. The "extermination of the infamy" foresaw the destruction of the Society of Jesus, the order founded by St. Ignatius against which the Enlightenment thinkers waged mortal combat, allying themselves with heterodox

74 Jean-Marie Goulemot, André Magnan, Didier Masseau, *Inventaire Voltaire*, Gallimard (Quarto), Paris 1995, "*Écrlinf*," p. 456.

75 Voltaire, *Oeuvres complètes*, vol. 10, Desoer, Paris 1817, p. 562.

76 Ibid., vol. 72, Imprimerie de Cosson, Paris 1827, p. 124.

77 Ibid., p. 79.

78 Cit. in André Magnan, *Penser l'infâme* [*Thinking Infamy*] "Cahiers Voltaire," Société Voltaire et Centre international d'étude du XVIIIe siècle, Paris 2014, p. 17 (pp. 7–50).

currents that were spreading within the Church.[79] The Jansenists who criticized the Jesuits for their lax morality thus found themselves in alliance with Enlightenment libertines, deniers of all morality, in convergence against a common enemy.

A typical strategy of conspirators is to accuse their victim of crimes they themselves are committing. In Europe reigned the so-called "enlightened despots," absolute sovereigns who drank deep at the well of Enlightenment ideas. The philosophical party convinced them that the Jesuits represented an obstacle to royal absolutism. Those conspiring against the monarchy accused of conspiracy those defending the sovereigns.

Some of these sovereigns decided to expel the Jesuits from their kingdoms, accusing them of perverting social order. The first attack against them was launched in 1759 by the Marquis of Pombal (1699–1782), the minister of King Joseph I of Portugal (1714–1777). After a series of defamatory libels, the Jesuits were accused of involvement in a plot against King Joseph and were expelled from Portugal, Brazil, and Goa. Following these expulsions were those carried out by the Bourbon sovereigns of Spain, France, and the Kingdom of Naples.

This was not enough, however. The Viscount Louis de Bonald (1754–1840) wrote that Enlightenment philosophy, nursing "the plan to tear down altar and throne in our homeland," considered it impossible to succeed in this plan without the demise of the Society of Jesus, "whose destruction was necessary as the firmest refuge of Throne and Altar, that they wished to shatter."[80] The occasion presented itself at the death of Pope Clement XIII on February 2,

[79] Cf. Enrico Rosa, S.J., *I Gesuiti dalle origini ai nostri giorni* [*The Jesuits from the Beginnings to Our Days*], La Civiltà Cattolica, Rome 1957, pp. 263–91.

[80] Louis de Bonald, *Risposta a nuove offese contro una celebre Compagnia* [*Response to New Offenses Against a Famous Company*], tr. It. Tip. Galeati, Imola 1827.

1769. In the sixteenth volume of his *History of the Popes,* Baron Ludwig von Pastor (1854–1928) describes with rich documentation the maneuvers conducted before, during, and after the conclave that, after three full months and 179 ballots, saw the election on May 14, 1769, of the Franciscan Lorenzo Ganganelli, with the name Clement XIV (1769–1774).

Historians still debate whether Cardinal Ganganelli had formally committed to suppressing the Jesuits or if he had limited his action to generic assurances. Nevertheless, on July 21, 1773, with the papal brief *Dominus ac Redemptor,* the new pope suppressed the Society of Jesus. This brief, writes Pastor, "represents the most obvious victory of the Enlightenment and royal absolutism over the Church and her Head."[81] "All observers," notes Joseph de Maistre (1753–1821), "were in agreement in considering the European Revolution (called the French Revolution), would have been impossible without the preliminary destruction of the Jesuits."[82]

With the constitution *Sollicitudo omnium ecclesiarum* of August 7, 1814, Pope Pius VII (1799–1823) revoked the Brief of 1773 and ordered the complete reconstitution of the Society of Jesus, "seeming to him a grave fault before God if in such a calamitous time we were further to withhold from the barque of the Church those capable and expert rowmen."[83]

13. French Revolution and Regicide

The French Revolution, which broke out in 1789, marked the symbolic passage from the epoch of *congiure* to that of conspiracies.

[81] L. von Pastor, *Storia dei Papi* [*History of the Popes*], cit., vol. XVI, 2, p. 223.

[82] Joseph de Maistre, Letter of June 26, 1816, in *Lettres et opuscules inédits,* A. Vaton, Paris 1853, vol. II, p. 316.

[83] L. von Pastor, *Storia dei Papi* [*History of the Popes*], cit., vol. XVI, 2, p. 421.

In 1649, King Charles I of England (1625–1649) was decapitated under the accusation of high treason. He was the first monarch in history to be condemned to death by a court, but as a traitor to Parliament, not as king, as Oliver Cromwell declared.[84] The death of the King Louis XVI of France on January 21, 1793, on the other hand, was the institutionalization of ideological assassination.

On September 21, 1792, the Revolutionary Convention proclaimed the decadence of monarchy and in the month of December decreed that "the citizen Louis Capet" would be tried. Upon Marat's proposal, it was also decided that during the trial all voting would be held by manifest nominal appeal. The debate lasted from December 27, 1792, until January 6, 1793, and on January 15 they began the vote. The sovereign was unanimously declared guilty of conspiring against liberty: his crime was that of having reigned. The following day, roll call was held over the crucial problem: "What sentence to inflict upon Louis Capet?" Each member of parliament approached the rostrum to justify his vote. After a first round, contested by a group of deputies, on January 18, the Convention expressed its definitive sentence: Louis XVI was condemned to death with 361 votes in favor and 360 against. Each deputy who had cast his vote for death had on his conscience the determining vote.

Msgr. Jean-Joseph Gaume (1802–1879) reported some of the declarations by which the Convention deputies decreed the death of King Louis[85]:

[84] "It was not due to the fact that he was king that the king's head must roll," Cromwell had declared to the aldermen of London in 1653 (Michael Walzer, *Régicide et Révolution: The Trial of Louis XVI; Speeches and Controversies* [*Regicide and Revolution. The trial of Louis XVI. Speeches and controversies*], tr. Fr. Payot, Paris 1989 [1974], p. 123).

[85] Msgr. Jean-Joseph Gaume, *La Révolution. Recherches historiques sur l'origine et la propagation du mal en Europe* [*The Revolution: Historical Research into*

- ✠ Louis Fréron (1754–1802): "I ask that before pronouncing the jail sentence, the image of Brutus be veiled and his bust be taken out of here: I vote for death."
- ✠ Louis Louchet (1753–1815): "If the opinion of those who vote for incarceration or banishment should prevail, I support the motion made by Fréron to remove from here the image of Brutus: I vote for death."
- ✠ Jean-Henri Vouland (1751–1801): "I ask for Louis the same torture inflicted by Brutus upon his sons: I vote for death."
- ✠ Denis-Marie Pélissier (1765–1829): "Brutus, the great man whose effigy I see here, overthrew the tyrant of Rome, without giving reasons: I vote for death."
- ✠ Jean Guillaume Taillefer (1764–1835): "Trembling, I apply the law that brings to death one similar to me, but my eyes are fixed on the image of the one who liberated Rome from tyranny: I vote for death."

Jean-Pierre-André Amar (1755–1816): "The death of Louis is necessary — I swear upon Brutus and vote for death."

It was in Brutus's name that Louis XVI was condemned to death and guillotined on January 21, 1793. It was a downright "Brutus Syndrome," as defined by the American historian Robert L. Herbert (1929–2020), finding echo in the admiration of humanists for the ancient pagans.[86]

According to Michael Walzer, who justifies the Jacobins, "public regicide" is "the founding action of the new regime."[87] The French Revolution did not want to punish the criminal in Louis XVI, but the

---

the Origin and Spread of Evil in Europe], Gaume frères, Paris 1856, vol. I, pp. 244–45.

86 Robert L. Herbert, *Voltaire, Brutus and the French Revolution: An Essay in Art and Politics*, Viking Press, New York 1973, p. 53.

87 M. Walzer, *Régicide et Révolution*, cit., p. 22.

sovereign: what was on trial was not the man but the monarchical institution as such, and behind that institution, a principle, namely the Catholic monarchy. For this reason, Pius VI (1775–1799) applies to the death of Louis XVI the term "martyrdom."[88]

The idea of a divine legitimacy of royalty was overturned by the affirmation of Saint-Just (1767–1794) at the Convention, "One cannot reign in innocence: this absurdity is all too evident. Every king is a rebel and a usurper."[89] "The mere qualification of king," stated Robespierre (1758–1794), "attracts the scourge of war upon the dismayed nation: neither prison nor exile can render his existence indifferent to the public happiness."[90] In fact, royalty "is an eternal crime against which every man has the right to rebel and take up arms: it is one of those aggressions which could not even be justified by the blinding of the entire population."[91]

The French Revolution, observes the philosopher Henri Beausoleil, was under this aspect a "long regicide,"[92] in which King Louis slowly became hostage, then victim of the new power. Every trace of the French monarchy had to be obliterated. The Convention, after the killing of Louis XVI and Queen Marie Antoinette, ordered the destruction of the tombs in the royal necropolis of Saint-Denis, where the bodies of the kings and queens of France were profaned. That took place in the months of August and October of 1793.

88 Pio VI, allocuzione *Quare Lacrymae* of June 17, 1793, in *Bullarii Romani Continuatio*, vol. VI, parte III, Tipografia Aldina, Prato 1849, pp. 2627–37.

89 Louis-Antoine de Saint-Just, Discourse of November 13, 1792, in *Archives parlementaires de la Révolution française*, Paul Dupont, Paris 1898, vol. 53, p. 391.

90 Maximilien de Robespierre, Discourse of December 3, 1792, in *Archives parlementaires*, cit., vol. 54, pp. 76–77.

91 Ibid.

92 Henri Beausoleil, *La mort de Louis XVI* [*The Death of Louis XVI*], in *Le Livre noir de la Révolution française* Éditions du Cerf, Paris 2009, p. 110 (pp. 95–136).

14. The Political Assassination Attempts of the Nineteenth Century

The regicides of the 1800s recalled the principle sanctioned by the Revolutionary Convention of 1793. "He did not kill Umberto, he killed the king," declared Gaetano Bresci, confirming the ideological nature of the assassination by gunshot of the Italian King Umberto I, on July 29, 1900, in Monza.[93] In 1820, the Duke of Berry, son of King Charles X of France, fell victim to revolutionary secret societies, as did Pellegrino Rossi, Pious IX's prime minister. In 1875, President Gabriel Garcia Moreno of Ecuador was assassinated, while in 1858, Emperor Napoleon III miraculously escaped the bombs planted by Felice Orsini. The conspiracies and the assassination attempts that occurred were not born of palace *congiure* or court intrigues, but were the fruit of an ideological and political choice.

If in the era of the *congiure* (from 1400 to 1800) political crimes were often concealed, during the 1800s, anarchists theorized the assassination of rulers as a public, demonstrative gesture. Revolutionary anarchists and socialists like Carlo Pisacane (1818–1857) opposed the propaganda of ideas with what they called propaganda of deeds, or propaganda with deeds, because as Pisacane stated, "ideas are the result of deeds, and not the former of the latter, and the people will not be free because they are educated, but will be educated when they shall be free."[94]

Expelled from the First International Workingmen's Association due to the intrigues of the followers of Karl Marx (1818–1883), the anarchists, following the exhortations of their leaders, formed an Anarchist International and dedicated themselves to

93 Carlo Capuano, *Detenuto 515. Bresci, ideologia di un regicida* [*Prisoner 515: Bresci, Ideology of a Regicide*], Zambon, Milan 2013, p. 27.

94 Carlo Pisacane, *Testamento politico* [*Political Testiment*], in *Saggio sulla Rivoluzione*, Libreria Treves, Bologna 1894, p. 267.

organizing, according to the formula of Peter Kropotkin (1842–1921), "the permanent revolt by means of the word, writing, the knife, the gun, and dynamite."[95] In the *Revolutionary Catechism* (1869) of Sergei Nechaev (1847–1882), which would exert a profound influence on the young Lenin,[96] the revolutionary was seen as a priest of slaughter: "The revolutionary is like a man who has taken vows. He ought to have but one interest, but one thought, but one passion: Revolution.... He has one objective, one science: destruction.... Between him and society there is a war to the last drop of blood, incessant, irreconcilable.... He must make a list of those condemned to death and carry out their sentences according to the order of their relative iniquity."[97]

With ruthless consistency, anarchists bloodied all of Europe from the end of the nineteenth century to the beginning of the twentieth century, organizing hundreds of rebellions and assassination attempts. Under the blows of anarchists fell President Sadi Carnot France (1894), Empress Elisabeth of Austria (1898), King Umberto I of Italy (1900), and President William McKinley of the United States (1901). In 1881, the Russian Czar Alexander II was assassinated by the secret populist association called Narodnaya Volya, meaning the People's Will, whose ideas were later taken up by the Socialist Revolutionary Party, an important faction in the revolutions of 1905 and 1917.

The death that struck international public opinion more than any other was that of the Austrian Empress Elisabeth of Wittelsbach, called Sissi, which occurred on September 10, 1898. It was the Italian

95 Pyotr Kropotkin, in *Il Rivoltoso* [*The Uprising*], Geneva, December 25, 1880.

96 Alain Besançon, *Le origini intellettuali del leninismo* [*The Intellectual Origins of Leninism*], tr. It. Sansoni, Florence 1978, pp. 111–25.

97 Cit. in George Woodcock, *L'anarchia. Storia delle idee e dei movimenti libertari* [*Anarchy: A History of Libertarian Ideas and Movements*], tr. It. Feltrinelli, Milan 1980, p. 151.

anarchist Luigi Lucheni who killed her in Geneva with a file used as a dagger. In the early years of the twentieth century, there followed the assassinations of King Alexander of Serbia and his wife Draga Maši, killed by a group of army officers on June 11, 1903; Carlos I of Portugal, victim together with his son Luis Filipe, on February 1, 1909, by a republican plot; and George I of Greece, assassinated on March 18, 1913, by the anarchist Alexandros Schinas.

In 1903, a gifted Jesuit theologian, Fr. Salvatore Brandi (1852–1913), published in *Civiltà Cattolica*, a study titled "Italians in the Statistics of Regicide" in which he noticed with great exactitude seventy-three regicides carried out in the space of one hundred years, between 1801 and 1903, of which eighteen were actually committed and fifty-five were merely attempted.[98] The statistics debunked the idea that Italians had the primacy of these bloody crimes: "The horrible plant of regicide is not indigenous to Italy; it prospers everywhere."[99]

15. The Consequences of Terror

The regicidal assassination attempts are, on the individual level, what genocide is on the collective level. Both are fruits of the culture of Terror of the French Revolution.

Historians usually circumscribe the period of the Terror from June or July of 1793 to July 28, 1794, the date of Robespierre's death. This was the period of the Jacobin Convention, after the elimination of the Girondins, when the Terror was placed on the order of business and then theorized by Saint-Just and Robespierre.

98 Salvatore Brandi, "Gli italiani nella statistica del regicidio" [Italians in the Statistics of Regicide], in *Civiltà Cattolica*, fasc. 1623, January 27, 1903, pp. 257–70.

99 Ibid., p. 263.

A member of the Revolutionary Tribunal, Pierre-Antoine Antonelle (1747–1817), confided that according to Robespierre, "it was necessary to exterminate all those who preferred the preceding form of government," and that they could never reach a democratic and egalitarian regime "if a third of the population was not first suppressed."[100]

In this period, the Revolutionary Tribunal and its emissaries in the provinces killed perhaps more than 20,000 people including exponents of the nobility, the clergy and political opponents, presumed traitors and suspects. Consistent with this plan of depopulating France, a genocide on a vast scale was conducted in the Vendée, in which nearly 117,000 inhabitants were indiscriminately murdered.[101] In the face of the military successes of the counter-revolutionary insurrection in the western regions of France, the Convention decided to exterminate several "brigands of the Vendée," sending against the rebels the punitive military expedition called the "Infernal Column," whose objective was to prevent "anything from escaping the national revenge."

Added to the civil war within France was the war declared by France on April 20, 1792, against the other European powers in order to export the Revolution. This war would last, with a number of brief intervals, for more than twenty-three years, until the definitive fall of Napoleon on June 22, 1815. Thus was born, as observed the German philosopher Roman Schnur (1927–1996), the European Civil War.[102] This conflict erupted as a consequence

[100] Cit. in Nesta Webster, *Democrazia e Terrore nella Rivoluzione francese* [*Democracy and Terror in the French Revolution*], tr. It. Ffede e Cultura, Verona 2020, p. 481.

[101] Cf. Reynald Secher, *La Vendée-Vengé: le génocide franco-français* [*Vendée-Vengé: The Franco-French Genocide*], Presses Universitaires de France, Paris 1986.

[102] Roman Schnur, *Rivoluzione e guerra civile* [*Revolution and Civil War*], tr. It. Giuffrè, Milan 1986, pp. 56–88.

of the ideological fanaticism denounced by Edmund Burke (1729–1797) in his celebrated *Reflections on the Revolution in France*, wherein he foresaw that a "gang of assassins" would have brought into the world a new type of war, profoundly different from previous ones.[103]

The epoch which opened with the French Revolution was destined to be the cruelest epoch in history, but also, as we shall see, the shadiest, due to the role it carried out in the revolutionary process of the nineteenth and twentieth centuries by secret societies and their conspiracies.

[103] Edmund Burke, *Reflections on the Revolution in France*, J. Dodsley, London 1790.

CHAPTER TWO

Conspiracies and Secret Societies

1. Freemasonry and Its Precursors

The Italian term *congiura* and the English word *conspiracy* betray a subtle but decisive difference. While *congiure* are secret agreements, limited to a few people and aimed at suppressing a sovereign or a politician, for reasons often tied to power, conspiracies are broader in scope and propose the overthrow of the constituted order. Conspirators are almost always revolutionaries; those involved in *congiure* are not necessarily so. The golden age of *congiure* spans approximately from 1400 to 1800. With the Enlightenment and the French Revolution, an age dawns in which conspiracies of an ideological and political character develop alongside traditional *congiure*.

The French Revolution was prepared by the "Republic of Letters" of the Enlightenment philosophers, and this was preceded and facilitated by Freemasonry, whose emergence marks the passage from the epoch of the *congiure* to that of conspiracies.

Freemasonry was born as a secret society internal to the construction guilds among artisans (architects, bricklayers, foremen). The name "lodge," which indicates the places where the meetings of the "brothers" are held, comes from architectural language, and was used to express the passage of Freemasonry from an "operative" association, of a professional nature, to a "speculative" society, of an ideological character. This happened on June 24, 1717, when four operative lodges existing in various neighborhoods in London united to form one large speculative lodge, the Grand Lodge of England, destined to become the mother lodge of world Freemasonry. This was the historical moment that witnessed the victory of Protestantism in Northern Europe and the ascension to the throne of the House of Hanover, which succeeded the Stuarts in 1714 as the reigning house of Great Britain and Ireland. The power of the English kingdom aided the rapid diffusion of the new institution, which, by mid-century, had penetrated all the principal countries in Europe.

The first official document of Freemasonry dates back to 1723: these are the *Constitutions* of James Anderson (1679–1739), a Scottish Presbyterian pastor nominated "Grand Master" of the Grand Lodge of London. This document affirms that Freemasons are obliged only "to the religion suitable to all men, leaving to each his opinions."[104] Freemasonry, therefore, presented itself from its very beginnings as an ideology that consists in placing aside every religious and moral truth, reducing traditional religions to subjective opinions. In this sense, relativism constitutes the soul of Freemasonry, although it does not include its entire essence. Freemasonry, in fact, presumes to be a "universal religion," a depository of a secret of which the freemason becomes gradually aware through the rites, symbols, and texts he assimilates, but also by means of the engaging atmosphere he breathes in his lodge.[105]

In the first half of the 1700s, Freemasonry was already structured in three fundamental degrees: Apprentice, Fellowcraft, and Master, each with its own initiation ceremony, which the Anglican priest (later a convert to Catholicism) Walton Hannah (1912–1966) described in detail based on the original texts. By means of these rituals, "one can

[104] James Anderson, *Le Costituzioni dei Liberi Muratori 1723* [*The Constitutions of the Freemasons 1723*], tr. It. Bastogi, Ffoggia 1991, p. 92.

[105] Padre Paolo M. Siano, FI, *Un Manuale per conoscere la Massoneria* [*A Manual to Know the Freemasons*], Casa Mariana, Frigento (AV) 2012, pp. 29–30.

ascertain how Freemasonry presents itself as a self-sufficient system of spiritual and moral guidance for this world and for the next."[106] The rite of admission to the degree of Master, which represents the fulfilment of the previous degrees, commemorates the assassination of Hiram, the chief architect of the workers sent to Jerusalem by the King of Tyre to construct the Temple. The member is subjected to what the Freemasons define as a "psychodrama"[107]: after having been symbolically struck, he is covered with a funerary drapery and laid in a coffin, from which he "rises" to enter into supreme knowledge.

The first three degrees were superimposed by systems of Masonic High Degrees called "Rites," characterized by magical and cabalistic content such as the Ancient and Accepted Scottish Rite of Freemasonry, with its structure of thirty-three degrees. Not all the members of the Freemasons know its final goals, which are understood only by the initiates of the highest degrees, who swear under pain of death not to reveal them. However, behind the various rites and obedience, there exists the same conception of the world, diametrically opposed to that of the Catholic Church.

The Freemasons claim their initiation rites are tied in a more or less legendary way to the Order of Templars, suppressed in 1313, and with the elusive Rosicrucians of the 1600s. We shall not enter these debates in which history overlaps with fiction, and we advise reading the concise and balanced essay dedicated to *Les précurseurs de la Franc-Maçonnerie,*[108] by the economics professor Claude Jannet

[106] Walton Hannah, *Visible Darkness: A Revelation and Interpretation of Freemasonry*, Augustine Publishing, Devon 1980, p. 40.

[107] Hiram, in *Dictionnaire de la Franc-Maçonnerie* [*Dictionary of the French Freemasons*], ed. by Daniel Ligou, P.U.F., Paris 1974, p. 585. On this necromantic rite, see also P. M. Siano, *Un Manuale per conoscere la Massoneria* [*A Manual to Know the Freemasons*], cit., pp. 60–68.

[108] Claude Jannet, *Les précurseurs de la Franc-Maçonnerie au XVI et XVII siècle* [*The Precursors of Freemasonry in the Sixteenth and Seventeenth Centuries*], V. Palmé, Paris 1887, reprinted by Éditions Saint-Rémy in 2011.

(1844–1894), who completed and republished the fundamental work of Fr. Nicolas Deschamps, *Les sociétés secrètes et la société* (1882).[109] After having recalled the doctrinal affinities of Freemasonry with the ancient heresies of the Gnostics and the Manicheans, Jannet offers us a precise historical reconstruction of the origins of Freemasonry from the sixteenth to the eighteenth century. His work concludes in these words: "Before Freemasonry enveloped Christian Europe with its network and prepared the explosion of 1789, . . . various groups, animated by a profound hatred toward Christianity, lived disseminated and hidden under a thick veil of hypocrisy and transmitted the traditions of the ancient heresies. The lodges gave these hostile forces an organization appropriate to the spirit of the age and to the corruption of the upper classes, while in their infinitely varied rituals, they gathered and blended all of the errors of the past, uniting them in that great negation of God's governance and rights that is naturalism."[110]

Fr. François Lefranc (1733–1792) of the Congregation of Jesus and Mary (the Eudists), martyred in the massacres of September during the French Revolution and beatified by Pius XI in 1926, was perhaps the first to connect the Freemasons to the Collegia Vicentina, a secret group of heretics who, in the name of the relativizing principle, dissolved all Catholic dogmas beginning with the Trinity.[111] The more radical wing within their ranks was represented by

[109] Nicholas Deschamps, *Les sociétés secrètes et la société, ou philosophie de l'histoire contemporaine (1874–1876)* [*Secret Societies and Society, or Philosophy of Contemporary History (1874–1876)*], Oudin Frères, Paris 1882. On the Gnostic and templar origins of Freemasonry see Paul Benoît, *La Franc-Maçonnerie et les sociétés secrètes* [*Freemasonry and Secret Societies*], 2 vol., Société Générale Catholique, Paris 1886, vol. I, pp. 23–62.

[110] C. Jannet, *Les précurseurs de la Franc-Maçonnerie au XVI et XVII siècle* [*The Precursors of Freemasonry in the Sixteenth and Seventeenth Centuries*], pp. 64–65.

[111] François Lefranc, *Voile levé (pour le curieux) ou l'histoire de la franc-maçonnerie depuis son origine jusqu'à nos jours* [*Sails Up for the Curious: The History of Freemasonry from Its Origins to the Present Day*], Lepetit et Guillemard, Paris 1792.

the Sociniani, who took their name from Lelio Socini (1525–1562) of Siena, and then from his nephew Fausto (1539–1604) of whom Fr. Lefranc recalls the epitaph placed on his tomb in Krakow: "*Tota licet Babylon destruxit tecta Lutehrus, muros Calvinus, sed fundamenta Socinus.*" If Luther destroyed the roof of the Catholic Church (referred to as Babylon), and if Calvin ruined its walls, Socini could boast of having ripped up the foundations. Fausto Socini, according to Lefranc, not only wanted to destroy the Church, but sought to erect a new religious temple and his disciples used the symbols adapted to this goal: aprons, triangles, and compasses.

The Sociniani profess anti-trinitarianism or unitarianism, because they deny the divinity of the Holy Spirit and affirm that Jesus Christ was only a man. They deny the existence of original sin, the necessity of Redemption in Christ, of grace, and of the sacraments, considered mere symbols, beginning with the Eucharist. With these doctrines Protestantism overturned the premises on which it began. If Luther had proclaimed the principle of "sola fide," the Sociniani proclaimed that of "only reason," submitting the Sacred Scriptures to a rationalist desecration.[112]

Between the seventeenth and the eighteenth centuries, Socinianism spread throughout the Low Countries and England, not as a confession, but as a mentality, contributing to the birth of Deism, whose inspiring principle was the distinction between natural and revealed religion. The "rational religion" of Deism coincides with that of Freemasonry, which reduces God to a generic "Supreme Being" or "Great Architect of the Universe." The relationship of Socinianism with Freemasonry can be followed through the figure of the Deist philosopher John Toland (1670–1722), author of a work

[112] R. de Mattei, *A sinistra di Lutero. Sette religiose del Cinquecento* [*To the Left of Luther: Religious Sects of the Fifteenth Century*], Solfanelli, Chieti 2017, pp. 94–101, 179–82.

titled *Pantheisticon* (1720), in which he illustrated the doctrine and organization of "Socratic societies" that present themselves as centers not only of philosophical and political discussion, but also of initiation to pantheism, proposing to its adherents the realization of an egalitarian republic free of every form of "religious superstition."[113] Toland was an admirer and disciple of Baruch Spinoza (1632–1677), whose Pantheistic-Naturalistic philosophy destroyed the theological notion of sin and the ethical notion of good and evil.[114]

Voltaire (pen name of François-Marie Arouet: 1694–1778), who lived in England from 1726 to 1728, was the great popularizer in France of these ideas, which constituted the cultural background of the Revolution of 1789.

2. Freemasonry and the French Revolution

The role of Freemasonry in the French Revolution was demonstrated by scholars such as Gustave Bord (1852–1934),[115] while another French historian of the highest caliber, Augustin Cochin (1876–1916), in his classic *La Révolution et la libre-pensée*, published posthumously in 1924, analyzed the thought societies that frequented Freemasonry and formed a network dependent on the Club of Jacobins.[116] There

113 Margaret C. Jacob, *The Newtonians and the English Revolution*, Cornell University Press, Ithaca 1976, p. 248. Cf. John Toland, *Pantheisticon*, ed. by Onofrio Nicastro and Manlio Iofrida, tr. It. Edizioni Ets, Pisa 1996.

114 Paul Siwek, *Spinoza et le panthéisme religieux* [*Spinoza and Religious Pantheism*], Desclée de Brouwer, Paris 1937; Andrea Dalledonne, *Il rischio della libertà: S. Tommaso–Spinoza* [*The Risk of Freedom: St. Thomas–Spinoza*], Marzorati, Milan 1990, pp. 103–182.

115 Gustave Bord, *La franc-maçonnerie en France des origines à 1815* [*Freemasonry in France from Its Origins to 1815*], Nouvelle Librairie Nationale, Paris 1908.

116 Cf. Augustin Cochin, *Meccanica della Rivoluzione* [*Mechanics of Revolution*], tr. It. Rusconi, Milan 1974, e *Lo spirito del giacobinismo* [*The Spirit of Jacobism*], tr. It. Bompiani, Milan 1981.

was no place in France on the eve of the Revolution that did not have its circle of freethinkers, its patriotic society, its lodge.

These studies were reproposed by Bernard Faÿ (1893–1978) in his work *Freemasonry and the Intellectual Revolution of the Eighteenth Century*. In 1789, according to Faÿ, "more than six hundred regular accepted lodges functioned in France: sixty-five in Paris, four hundred forty-two in the provinces, thirty-nine in the colonies, sixty-nine in the regiments, and seventeen abroad."[117] "Freemasonry in the eighteenth century gave rise to the revolutionary spirit, the revolutionary spirit gave rise to revolutions and revolutions gave rise to a new Freemasonry."[118]

In 1773, Duke Louis Philippe II of Orleans (1747–1793) became Grand Master of the Grand Orient of France, and at court fierce competition to follow his example became the rule in what Faÿ termed "the Masonic suicide of the high nobility."[119] The Palais Royal, the property of the House of Orleans, became on the eve of the Revolution the center of all political and social agitators, although Gustav Bord is not wrong in stating that the Duke was only the visible head of Freemasonry and that the members of the sect used him to cover their designs, while he and his supporters used the others with the same objective.[120]

The lodge of *Les Neufs Sœurs* was the most influential of the French lodges on the eve of the Revolution. Among its members, besides Voltaire, was Benjamin Franklin (1706–1790), who had arrived in Paris as a diplomatic representative of the United States, Antoine Court de Gébelin (1725–1784), the inventor of the science of Tarot cards, Ignace Joseph Guillotin (1738–1814), the inventor of the

117 Bernard Faÿ, *La Massoneria e la Rivoluzione intellettuale del secolo XVIII* [*Freemasonry and the Intellectual Revolution of the Eighteenth Century*], tr. It. Einaudi, Turin 1939, p. 249.

118 Ibid., p. 282.

119 Ibid., p. 266–71.

120 G. Bord, *La conspiration révolutionnaire de 1789* [*The Revolutionary Conspiracy of 1789*], Bibliothèque d'Histoire Moderne, Paris 1909, pp. 32–33.

guillotine, and Count Honoré de Mirabeau (1749–1791), a high-level Mason who, in 1791, was elected president of the National Assembly.

The French Revolution was the result of the convergence of different interests and objectives, against the backdrop of the profound transformation of ideas and traditions of the eighteenth century. Within the Masonic lodges, an optimistic spirit of faith in progress which longed for the end of traditional religion was widespread, but not the French monarchy. The intention of the Duke of Orleans and of his party was to change the dynastic house, not to topple the monarchy. Furthermore, if all supporters of Orleans were Freemasons, not all Freemasons were supporters of Orleans. Not the fall but the weakening of the monarchy was the aim of the diplomatic intrigues of Prussia, who wanted to break the Franco-Austrian alliance. The destruction of Throne and Altar, in France and in Europe, was a secret objective shared only by a few of high degree in Freemasonry and of a secret society that had developed within it: the Bavarian Illuminati.

3. The Bavarian Illuminati and the Convent of Wilhelmsbad

The Bavarian Illuminati or, more precisely, the Order of the Illuminati, was founded in 1776 by Adam Weishaupt (1748–1830), professor of canon law at the University of Ingolstadt. The objective of the sect, revealed only to the initiates of the upper degrees, was to destroy religions, overthrow governments, and abolish private property. Weishaupt, according to the liberal-socialist historian Carlo Francovich (1910–1990), "nourished in his soul the ideas of an atheistic materialism, imagining as the final destiny of human existence an egalitarian, anarchical society."[121] In 1786, the police of

[121] Carlo Francovich, *Storia della Massoneria in Italia, dalle origini alla Rivoluzione francese* [*History of Freemasonry in Italy, from the Origins of the French Revolution*], La Nuova Italia, Florence 1989, p. 310.

Duke Karl Theodore of Bavaria discovered the conspiracy and sequestered extensive documentation, a carbon copy of which was sent to all the European courts. The *Abbé,* ex-Jesuit Augustin Barruel (1741–1820), came into possession of the documents, and published them in his *Mémoires pou servir à l'histoire du jacobinisme* (1798–1799), a work that was reprinted several times and translated into the main European languages.[122]

At the beginning of the 1900s, a non-Catholic historian of Freemasonry, René Le Forestier (1868–1951), scrupulously explored German archives finding full confirmation of what Barruel had written. The documents of the Bavarian Illuminati are held in three main depositories: the Secret Archives of the Royal House of Bavaria which conserve all the papers confiscated in the seizure and the transcripts of the interrogations; the Library of the University of Munich, and the Archives of the Lodge Ernst zum Compass of Gotha. These documents, both printed and handwritten, writes Le Forestier, "are abundant, certainly authentic" and "give certain and precise information about the doctrine and destinies of the association, enabling one to shed light on the essential points."[123] Le Forestier continues, "Barruel read all of it. His numerous citations are translated in a somewhat weak manner, but they are faithful. From the mass of confused documents he collected, from the meticulous analysis of the original writings, he was able to make a complete account though slightly tendentious toward the organization, the order, and its history until its dissolution in Bavaria."[124]

122 Augustin Barruel, *Mémoires pour servir à l'histoire du jacobinisme* [*Memoirs for the History of Jacobism*], Hambourg, 5 vol., P. Fauche, Hamburg 1798–1799. The work was republished by La Diffusion de la Pensée Française, in 1974 and again in 2013, with an introduction by Christian Lagrave.

123 René Le Forestier, *Les Illuminés de Bavière et la franc-maçonnerie allemande* [*The Bavarian Illuminati and German Freemasonry*], Hachette, Paris 1914, p. 9.

124 Ibid., p. 687.

Paolo Bianchini, a scholar who recently examined the handwritten annotations of Barruel in *Mémoires pou servir à l'histoire du jacobinisme,*[125] verified the reliability of the sources he used in redacting the work, founded on first-hand documents and on hundreds of testimonies of well-known and well-informed people. The conspiracy of the Bavarian Illuminati has nothing to do with fiction; it was a reality.

In 1782, the Convention (or "convent") of Wilhelmsbad was held near Hanau in Germany. It constitutes "the only example of a universal attempt at organic, ritual, and doctrinal formulation of the Masonic Order."[126] In the German city, the most eminent representatives of the secret societies of Europe convened under the presidency of Prince Ferdinand of Brunswick (1721–1792), among numerous observers, in such a way as to form one of the most representative assemblies in the history of Freemasonry.[127]

Already from that time, the two tendencies that had characterized Protestantism were manifest in Freemasonry: the rationalist tendency and the Theosophic tendency. The rationalist tendency was represented by the Bavarian Illuminati, among whom were Christoph Bode (1731–1793) and Franz Dietrich von Dittfurth (1738–1813) representing Weishaupt. The Theosophic tendency belonged to the "Martinists," so-called because they were followers of Martinès de Pasqually (1727–1774) and Louis-Claude de Saint-Martin (1743–1803). In Wilhelmsbad, they were guided by Jean-Baptiste Willermoz (1730–1824) and by François-Henri de Virieu (1754–1793). The latter was to distance himself later from Freemasonry and revealed to

125 Paolo Bianchini, *Le annotazioni manoscritte di Augustin Barruel ai Mémoires pour servir à l'histoire du jacobinisme* [*The Annotated Manuscripts of Augustin Barruel to His Memoirs for a History of Jacobism*], in *Annali della Fondazione Luigi Einaudi*, XXXIII (1999), pp. 367–444.

126 C. Francovich, *Storia della Massoneria* [*History of Freemasonry*], p. 342.

127 A. Barruel, *Mémoires pour servir à l'histoire du jacobinisme* [*Memoirs for the History of Jacobism*], Diffusion de la Pensée Française, Chiré-en-Montreuil 2013, vol. II, p. 321.

Abbé Barruel that the secret societies plotted "a conspiracy so well hatched and so deep that it would have been difficult for religion and governments not to succumb."[128]

This confidence was confirmed by the memories of Count de Virieu, published in 1892 by the Marquis Charles-Albert Costa de Beauregard (1835–1909). According to a tradition conserved in his family, Virieu returned from Germany convinced that the Bavarian Illuminati had prepared a universal conflagration and responded to the Baron de Gilliers, who had asked him what tragic secrets he was bearing from Wilhelmsbad, with such a sad tone as to leave his friend shocked: "I shall not confide it to you, but I can only say that it is much more serious than you think. The conspiracy being plotted is so well hatched that for the monarchy and for the Church it will be, shall we say, impossible to escape."[129]

4. The Count of Cagliostro

The existence of two formations in which Freemasonry of the 1700s was divided was also revealed by Giuseppe Balsamo, known as Alessandro Cagliostro (1763–1795), in his forty-three meticulous interrogations he suffered in Rome, from January 1790 to April 4, 1791, after having been arrested by the Pontifical Police. A synthesis of the trial is collected in *Compendium of the Life and Actions of Giuseppe Balsamo*,[130] redacted by Msgr. Giovanni Barberi (1748–1821), on the

[128] A. Barruel, *Mémoires pour servir à l'histoire du jacobinisme* [*Memoirs for the History of Jacobism*], Diffusion de la Pensée Française, Chiré-en-Montreuil 2013, vol. II, p. 321.

[129] *Le roman d'un royaliste sous la Révolution: souvenirs du C.te de Virieu* [*The Novel of a Royalist During the Revolution: Memories of C.te de Virieu*], ed. by Charles-Albert Costa de Beauregard, Plon, Nourrit, Paris 1892, p. 44.

[130] *Compendium of the Life and Actions of Giuseppe Balsamo named the Count Cagliostro, taken from his trial held in Rome in the year 1790 and which can serve as a glimpse to know the character of the sect of the Freemasons*, Stamperia della Rev. Camera Apostolica, Rome 1791.

basis of documents of the Sacred Inquisition, conserved today in the National Library of Rome.[131] This work, printed in the first months of 1791, on the eve of the sentencing that condemned Giuseppe Balsamo to life in jail in the fortress of San Leo, is divided into four parts. In the first, a biographical profile of Giuseppe Balsamo is outlined; in the second, the author gives a brief history of Freemasonry in general, lingering in particular on the "Egyptian rite," which he founded; in the third, the activity of Cagliostro as emissary and organizer of the Freemasons is examined; in the fourth, finally, the Roman lodge discovered in that period is discussed.

Cagliostro distinguishes within the world of the Freemasons a "Strict Observance" and a "High Observance": the former, to which the so-called Illuminati belong, professes an absolute unbelief and has as its main objective the total destruction of the Catholic religion and of the monarchy; the second, with which he was affiliated, studies nature to perfect the Hermetic arts and the search for the philosophers' stone. In both cases one adheres to a blind obedience to "Superior Unknowns," committing oneself never to reveal the secrets communicated by them. As a true traveling salesman of the Masonic lodges, Cagliostro traveled all of Europe under various names, together with his wife Lorenza Feliciani, impersonating a doctor and a necromancer and selling love potions and youth elixirs. In the interrogations, he affirmed he was the depository and the head (with the title of Great *Cofto*) of an esoteric form of "Egyptian Freemasonry," with a cabalistic backdrop, whose rites the compiler of the *Compendium* describes in detail.

In the epoch preceding the French Revolution, in academies, in literary salons, and even on every street corner, a sort of more or less

[131] Collection of legal writings concerning the trial of G. B. called Alessandro Count of Cagliostro and of P. Francesco Giuseppe by S. Maurizio Cappuccino, before the Tribunal of the Holy Office in Rome, National Library of Rome, Fondo Vittorio Emanuele, ms. 245, I–XXXV.

imaginary "science" of initiation was being spread, such as the "animal magnetism" of Franz Anton Mesmer (1734–1815), the "physiognomics" of Johann Casper Lavater (1741–1801), the hypnotism and somnambulism of the Marquess Armand-Marie-Jacques de Puységur (1751–1825). This atmosphere of irrationalism excited spirits, nourishing the dream of demolishing the monarchy, or at least of transforming it, and emancipating it from the Catholic Church to which it was still profoundly tied.

5. The Three Lives of Moses Dobrushka

Another disturbing character from those years is Moses Dobrushka[132] (1753–1794), abundantly recounted for us by Gershom Scholem (1897–1982), the "Master of the Kabbalah" of the Hebrew University of Jerusalem.[133] In numerous studies, Scholem analyzed Sabbatianism, a Jewish messianic movement that takes its name from the cabalist Shabbetay Zevi (1626–1676). This religious current represents for Scholem "the central event of Jewish history on the threshold of modernity," because "shaking the traditional foundations, it opened the path to modern movements such as Jewish Illuminism (Haskalah), reformed Judaism and even secularism."[134] The inheritance of Sabbatianism was passed on in the eighteenth century to Frankism, thus denominated after its "prophet" Jacob Frank (1726–1791), another "messiah," active mainly in Poland and Austria on the eve of the French Revolution.

Frankism and Sabbatianism, according to Scholem, are expressions of a mystical nihilism that theorizes the abolition of every religious law and moral norm as a "way to redemption." "All

[132] Gershom Scholem, *Le tre vite di Moses Dobrushka* [*The Three Lives of Moses Dobrushka*], Adelphi, Milan 2014, p. 121.

[133] David Biale, *Il Maestro della Cabala. Vita di Gershom Scholem* [*The Master of the Kabbalah: The Life of Gershom Scholem*], Carocci, Rome 2019.

[134] Ibid., p. 119.

positive religions are only a garment that the believer wears, or better yet, must wear to traverse them and surpass them, regardless whether it is Judaism, or Islam or Christianity, and better yet, if as happened to Jakob Frank in the course of his life, all three of them are traversed."[135] Scholem recalls that it was "to Bakunin, the father of anarchism, that we owe the maxim: 'The power of destruction is a creative power.' One hundred years before, Frank had placed at the center of his own utopia the redemptive power of destruction. The battle for destruction, a pure and original form of anarchy, embraces all levels of our existence. The ascent is preceded by the path into the abyss."[136]

Moses (Levi) Dobrushka received from his family a Jewish and rabbinic education and was initiated into what the sectarians called the "secret of the [Sabbatian and Frankian] faith."[137] In 1775, consistent with the dissimulation theorized by these Talmudic settings, Moses Dobrushka converted to Catholicism and, having obtained a title to the nobility, became a paladin of the Enlightenment in Austria, under the name of Thomas von Schönfeld. He entered the Freemasons and was affiliated with the Bavarian Illuminati and with the Asian Brotherhood, an order of Freemasons with a Theosophic-cabbalistic orientation, presided by Prince Christian of Hesse-Darmstadt (1744–1836). Another adherent of the Asian Brotherhood, the Bavarian noble Hans Heinrich von Ecker und Eckhofen (1750–1790), represented this cabalistic tendency at the Convent of Wilhelmsbad of 1782. The documents of the mysterious Order of the Asian Brotherhood, partly handwritten and partly printed, are preserved in the Masonic archives in Hamburg, Copenhagen, and the Hague, and were consulted by Scholem and by

135 G. Scholem, *Le tre vite di Moses Dobrushka* [*The Three Lives of Moses Dobrushka*], p. 149.

136 Ibid.

137 Ibid., pp. 18–19.

another Israeli scholar, Jacob Katz[138] (1904–1998), revealing the nihilist doctrine inspired by Sabbatianism and Frankism.

After the outbreak of the French Revolution, Dobrushka settled in Strasbourg where he took the name Junius Frey and distinguished himself as one of the most important Jacobins of the city. On April 5, 1794, Frey was arrested for treason and espionage, condemned to death, and guillotined with Georges Danton (1759–1794) and his brother-in-law, the former friar François Chabot (1756–1794). Thus ended, at forty years of age, the life of a man who, according to Scholem, was a prisoner of his own contradictions: "Jew or integrated apostate? Esoteric cabbalist or illuminated rationalist? Jacobin or spy? The doubt remains, but for sure he was an authentic Frankist."[139]

6. A High-Level Initiate of the Secret Societies: "Doctor Falck"

Toward the end of 1781, the Marquess François de Chefdbien d'Armissan (1753–1849), known in the sectarian world as *Eques a Capite Galeato,* as he was about to participate in the Convent of Wilhelmsbad, received from the Marquess Charles-Pierre-Paul Savalette de Langes (1745–1797), founder of the Lodge of Philalèthes, a series of *fiches,* or "cards," concerning people whom he was to meet during the journey. This correspondence, of greatest interest for historians, was published in a formidable volume by Benjamin Fabre, pseudonym of Jean-Baptiste Guiraud (1866–1931), professor at the Faculty of Letters of Besançon and known as one of the greatest scholars of the Inquisition. In the original *fiches,* reproduced by Fabre, Savalette speaks insistently of a mysterious personage called "Falc."

[138] Jacob Katz, *Der Orden der Asiatischen Brüder* [*The Order of the Asian Brothers*], in *Zwischen Messianismus und Zionismus. Zur jüdischen Sozialgeschichte,* Jüdischer Verlag, Frankfurt am Main 1993.

[139] G. Scholem, *Le tre vite di Moses Dobrushka* [*The Three Lives of Moses Dobrushka*], p. 121.

In one *fiche*, for example, is found the testimony of the *Abbé* Fournié (Pierre Fournié: 1738–1827), a priest initiated into the Martinist Lodge, who writes of Falc: "He is a man on all accounts quite extraordinary. Some believe him to be the leader of all the Jews. . . . He is nearly unapproachable. In all of the sects of wisemen of the secret sciences, he passes for a superior man. Today he is in England. The Baron von Gleichen can give some good information about him."[140] The Baron Karl Heinrich von Gleichen (1733–1807), writes Savalette, "knows Falc. . . . In a word, he is one of our most educated friends."[141] In another *fiche*, the Baron Johann Christian von Waldenfels (1742–1796) is defined as "the most interesting man you and I could know," also because "he knows Falc and Wecter"[142] (referring to the Baron Carl Eberhard von Wächter [1746–1825], the Danish ambassador at Regensburg).

The occult personality that recurs insistently, appearing as a high-level initiate of the secret societies, was the rabbi cabalist Samual Jacob Hayyim (1710–1782), known also as "Doctor Falck," "Ba'al Shem of London." The title Ba'al Shem (Master of the Divine Name) was attributed, according to Gershom Scholem, to the scholars of Kabbalah who possessed the secret knowledge of the Tetragrammaton and worked "miracles" through rites and magic.[143]

Samuel Jacob Hayyim was probably born in Podolia, in modern Ukraine, but soon moved to Germany. Accused of witchcraft by the authorities of Westphalia in 1736, he was secretly the guest of the German count Alexander Leopold Anton von Rantzau

[140] Benjamin Fabre, *Un initié des sociétés secrètes supérieures «Franciscus, eques a capite galeato» 1753–1814*, La renaissance française, Paris 1913, tr. It. Arché, Milan 2003, p. 79.

[141] Ibid., p. 83.

[142] Ibid., p. 105.

[143] G. Scholem, *Ba'al Shem*, in *Encyclopaedia Judaica*, vol. III, Keter Publishing House, London and New York 2007, p. 9; ibid., *Kabbalah*, Times Book Co., New York 1974, pp. 272–74.

(1681–1747) in his castle in Holzminden. During this stay, the rabbi made several amazing magic experiments. The count's son, Georg Ludwig Albrecht von Rantzau (1714–1786), presents a detailed report of the operations of the "*Prince et Grand-Prêtre des Juifs*" in his *Memorie,* in which he made use of cabalist formulas and figures and of a hunting knife that he waved in the air.[144]

Sometime later the rabbi arrived in London, where he lived until his death under the name of "Doctor Falck." The laboratory/synagogue of Dr. Samuel Jacob Falck was located at Wellclose Square, near the dwelling of the Swedish visionary Emanuel Swedenborg (1688–1772).

Marsha Keith Schuchard, author of numerous studies on secret societies, offered a detailed documentation of the cabalist contacts and of the Masonic activities of the two characters, both affiliated with the Lodge of the Seven Degrees. Falck, according to Schuchard, was one of the "Incognito Superiors" of the Illuminated Freemasonry, secretly associated with radical Polish Sabbatianism, and "instructed Swedenborg in the cabalistic techniques of trances and sexual magic."[145] The historian Auguste Viatte (1901–1993), in a classic work dedicated to the occult sources of romanticism, likewise abundantly documented the dependence of Martinist Freemasonry on Swedenborg.[146]

According to the testimony of Baron von Gleichen, Duke Philipe of Orleans "had received in England from the renowned Falck-Scheck,

[144] *Mémoirs du comte de Rantzow [The Memoirs of Count Rantzow],* Pierre Mortier, Amsterdam 1791, p. 197 (pp. 197–223).

[145] Marsha Keith Schuchard, "The Secret Masonic History of Blake's Swedenborg Society," in *Blake: An Illustrated Quarterly,* 26 (Fall 1992), p. 40 (pp. 40–51); "Yeats and the Unknown Superiors: Swedenborg, Falk, and Cagliostro," in *Secret Texts: The Literature of Secret Societies,* ed. by Marie Roberts and Hugh Orms-by-Lennon, AMS, New York 1995.

[146] Auguste Viatte, *Les sources occultes du romantisme: illuminisme, théosophie, 1770–1820* [*The Occult Sources of Romanticism: Illuminism, Theosophy, 1770–1820*], Librairie Honoré Champion, Paris 1927.

Head Rabbi of the Jews,"[147] a talisman of lapis lazuli that, thanks to his powers, had helped the Duke come to power in France. Madame de la Croix (Geneviève de Jarente: 1718–1799), a French "prophetess" and disciple of Saint-Martin, considered this amulet evil and boasted of having pulverized it with her exorcism while it was on the Duke's chest. The duel between magicians, nevertheless, did not bring good fortune to "Philippe-Égalité," who instead of ascending the throne ended up on the guillotine on November 6, 1793.

David Rudermann, professor of Jewish history, is convinced of Samuel Jacob Hayyim-Franck's connections with the Sabbatians, defining him as an "enigma for scholars."[148] For the little we know of Dr. Falck, his doctrine and his practice were inspired by cabalist antinomianism, a labyrinth into which it is often more prudent not to venture for fear of losing oneself. But here we seem to find ourselves before one of those men whom Plinio Corrêa de Oliveira, in his private conversations, defined the "pioneer revolutionaries," the unknown apex of the revolutionary secret societies.

7. Philippe Buonarroti and the Perfect Sublime Masters

Connected to the Bavarian Illuminati were the ultra-Jacobin exponents of the French Revolution, among whom were François-Noël Babeuf, called "Gracchus" (1760–1797), a fanatical disciple of Robespierre, and his follower Philippe Buonarroti (1761–1836).

Babeuf attempted an insurrection in France known as the "Conspiracy of the Equals," with which he sought to overthrow the Directory and reintroduce the Jacobin Constitution of 1793, but failed

147 *Souvenirs de Charles-Henri Baron de Gleichen* [*Memories of Charles-Henri Baron de Gleichen*], Léon Techener, Paris 1868, p. 176.

148 David B. Ruderman, "Rabbi, Mystic, or Impostor? The Eighteenth-Century Ba'al Shem of London," in *Jewish Historical Studies*, 52/1 (2021), pp. 315–19.

and was guillotined. Buonarroti inherited the movement, telling the story of the affair in a book titled: *Conspiration pour l'égalité, dite de Babeuf* (1828).[149] Continuing Babeuf's work, Buonarroti founded the Perfect Sublime Masters in Geneva around 1818, a secret revolutionary society which drew on the program and organizational structure of the Bavarian Illuminati.

Armando Saitta (1919–1991), a historian trained in the Marxist historiographical tradition, rediscovered and published the papers of Philippe Buonarroti.[150] In the first degree of this secret society, he professed liberal ideas and the observance of religion; in the second degree, the adherent was initiated into a more radical republican doctrine, of which tyrannicide was a part; in the third degree, the final program of the sect was revealed, namely the establishment of a communist society, according to the egalitarian principles of Weishaupt and Babeuf. Buonarroti, a Freemason of the highest degree of the sectarian leadership of Geneva called the "Great Firmament," directed the secret societies that operated in Italy such as the Carboneria, the Alta Vendita, the Perfect Sublime Masters, the Adelfi, and the Federati, who conspired to unite the peninsula and republicanize it, freeing it from the pope and from Austria.

It was not until 1824 that the Austrian Empire acquired exact knowledge of the scope of the sectarian plans and of its true goals, but the discovery of the papers of the conspirator Alexandre Andryane (1797–1863) brought to light the vastness of the conspiracy. In that year, Klemens von Metternich (1773–1859), Chancelor of the Empire, presented a memorandum to the German princes gathered in Vienna, in which, on the basis of these documents, he described

[149] Philippe Buonarroti, *Conspiration pour l'égalité, dite de Babeuf* [*Babeuf's Conspiracy for Equality*], 2 vol., Éditions Sociales, Paris 1957 (1828).

[150] Armando Saitta, *Filippo Buonarroti. Contributi alla storia della sua vita e del suo pensiero* [*Filippo Buonarroti: Contributions to the History of His Life and Thought*], Storia e Letteratura, Rome 1950–1951.

the structure of the Perfect Sublime Masters, demonstrating how the order, which united Freemasonry, Adelphia, and Philadelphia, "was to be considered a composite and that it followed under every sort of form its main aim, namely widescale republicanizing."[151]

Two years earlier, at the Congress of the Holy Alliance which met in Verona from October 9 to October 14, 1822, Count Christian von Haugwitz (1752–1832), a participant at the Convent of Wilhelmsbad, presented a memorandum in which he confessed that the French Revolution and its regicide were the result of the action of secret societies with which he had been affiliated, reaching their highest degrees. The document was published by the German historian and diplomat Wilhelm Dorow (1790–1846) in 1840.[152] Metternich and Haugwitz were two statesmen devoted to their respective sovereigns in Austria and Prussia and well informed on the events of their times. To place in doubt their word would mean renouncing every form of historical research, often based on documents much more ephemeral than are their memoranda.

8. The Alta Vendita (1818-1847)

On May 20, 1846, while preparing to embark from Ancona on a journey to the Orient, the French historian Jacques Crétineau-Joly (1803–1875) was convoked to Rome by Pope Gregory XVI for a project of greatest importance. The pope had important documents delivered to the historian that had been sequestered by the pontifical police and letters of presentation for the King of Naples and for Metternich, entrusting Crétineau-Joly the task of writing a history of secret societies.

151 Fr. Ilario Rinieri translates the text of Metternich's memoirs almost litterally in his *Della vita e delle opere di Silvio Pellico* [*On the Life of Silvio Pellico*], Roux, Turin 1899, vol. II, pp. 23 ff.

152 Wilhelm Dorow, *Denkschriften und Briefe zur Charakteristik der Welt und Litteratur* [*Memorials and Letters on the Characteristics of the World and Litterature*], Duncker, Berlin 1838/1841, vol. 4 (1840), pp. 211–21.

The tumultuous course of the events that followed — the death of Gregory XVI and the election of Pius IX (1846–1878), the Roman Republic, the Pontifical Restoration, the ascension to the throne of Napoleon III — rendered impossible the compilation of this work. Part of the collected material was employed, however, by the French historian in the two volumes of *L'Église romaine en face de la Révolution* (1859), in which he revealed the existence of the Alta Vendita, a society that occupied a higher level in the sectarian world than the organizations of Mazzini and Buonarroti.[153] The work of Crétineau-Joly was approved by a brief of Pius IX and an official note from the Secretary of Latin Letters, Msgr. Fioravanti, attests the authenticity of the documents reproduced.[154]

The Alta Vendita was constituted by some forty members who hid behind pseudonyms, and was directed by Nubius, an Italian aristocrat living in Rome, where he enjoyed elevated social status. "Our final goal," recited the Permanent Secret Instruction given to members of the Alta Vendita in 1819, "is that of Voltaire and of the French Revolution: the annihilation forever of Catholicism and the Christian idea, that it shall continue to perpetuate if it remains standing on the ruins of Rome."

To attain this goal, the Alta Vendita proposed the takeover of ecclesiastical upper echelons and the acquisition of their collaboration, in an analogous way to what the lower levels of the Carboneria did with European sovereigns. "There is a thought that has always occupied men who aspire to universal regeneration; it is the thought

153 Cf. Jacques Crétineau-Joly, *L'Église romaine en face de la Révolution* [*The Roman Church in the Face of the Revolution*], 2 vol., Plon, Paris 1859 (the work was reprinted by Cercle de la Renaissance Française, Paris 1976, 2 vol.).

154 Ulysses Maynard, *Jacques Crétineau-Joly: sa vie politique religieuse et littéraire d'après ses mémoires, sa correspondance et autres documents inédits* [*Jacques Crétineau-Joly: his political, religious and literary life from his memoirs, correspondence and other unpublished documents*], Librairie Firmin Didot, Paris 1875, pp. 400–401.

of the liberation of Italy, from which the liberation of the entire world one fine day shall proceed, the fraternal republic and the harmony of humanity.... The pontificate of over sixteen hundred years is pertinent to the history of Italy. Italy cannot breathe, cannot move without the permission of the supreme pastor.... We cannot desire this state of matters, and so a remedy must be found to such a sad condition. The remedy has been found. The pope, whoever he might be, will never draw near to the secret societies; the secret societies must take the first step toward the Church, with the aim of winning them both. The toil we shall undertake is the work neither of a day, nor a month, nor a year: it might take many years, perhaps a century; in our ranks a soldier may die but the war continues.... What we must seek and await like the Jews await the Messiah, is a pope who will serve our purposes."[155]

Nubius passed away in Malta in 1846, perhaps poisoned. The decline of the Alta Vendita transpires from the final words of the letter to the conspirator "Gaetano": "Giuseppe Mazzini in Campidoglio! Nubius in Rupe Tarpea or in oblivion! Behold the dream that oppresses me, if chance were to fulfill your hopes."[156]

9. From Giuseppe Mazzini to Karl Marx

Giuseppe Mazzini (1805–1872) wanted to style himself the successor to Philippe Buonarroti, founding around 1830 *Giovine Italia*. This and other secret societies established by him proposed the inauguration of a republic in Italy, through the organization of a generalized revolutionary movement throughout the peninsula, utilizing irregular mobs, as well as regular troops of several states, such as Piedmont. "Neither pope, nor king!", "War on the papacy!", "War against kings!": these were the slogans

155 J. Crétineau-Joly, *L'Église romaine en face de la Révolution* [*The Roman Church in the Face of the Revolution*], vol. II, pp. 82–83.

156 Ibid., vol. II, p. 382.

of Mazzini and his followers.[157] All the various attempts at insurrection by these Mazzinians (the Savoyard uprising in 1834, the expedition of the Bandiera in 1844, the Milanese uprising in 1853, the revolts of 1857 in Livorno and Genoa, followed by the expedition in the south of Pisacane) failed miserably, and Mazzini took refuge in London where he remained for more than thirty years, with several parentheses, as when he took part as triumvir in the brief life of the Roman Republic (1849).

Enrico Verdecchia, in his book *The London of the Conspirators,* told the story of revolutionaries of every nationality who, from 1820 to 1905, arrived in the English capital after wandering through various countries and often after having been expelled from other European capitals. The house of Mazzini in Middleton Square was one of the meeting places of these conspirators. One of the most active financiers of Mazzinian movement was Moses Meyer Nathan (1799–1859), father of Ernesto Nathan (1845–1921), future Grand Master of Italian Freemasonry and mayor of Rome. The Italian Risorgimento was the work of secret Carbonari societies, but Freemasonry dominated the new Kingdom born on March 17, 1861. On November 20, 1859, the Ausonia lodge of Turin brought to life the Grande Oriente of Italy which in September of 1861 elected as first Grand Master the Italian ambassador in Paris, Costantino Nigra (1828–1907).

Over the course of sixty years, from 1861 until the advent of fascism, the Freemasons counted among their numbers four prime ministers (Agostino Depretis, Francesco Crispi, Giuseppe Zanardelli, and Alessandro Fortis), alongside hundreds of ministers, parliamentarians, officials, writers, and entrepreneurs.

This book by Verdecchia and many others show us the extension and the connections of the conspiring network that enveloped

[157] Ermanno Gruber, S.J., *Giuseppe Mazzini. Massoneria e Rivoluzione. Studio storico-critico* [*Giuseppe Mazzini: Freemasonry and Revolution; A Historical-Critical Study*], Desclée, Lefebvre & C., Rome 1901, p. 65.

Europe in the mid-nineteenth century, while anarchist and socialist movements were born clandestinely. In February of 1848, the red flag unfurled for the first time on the barricades. In that same year, the *Communist Manifesto* was published, authored by Karl Marx (1818–1883) and Friedrich Engels (1820–1895) on behalf of the *Bund des Gerichten* (League of the Righteous), a secret revolutionary society founded by Wilhelm Weitling (1808–1871), later transformed into the Communist League.[158]

After the experience of 1848, the First International was formed in 1864 in London, the main protagonists in the early days being Marx and the anarchist Mikhail Bakunin (1814–1876). The Paris Commune of 1871 represented a new revolutionary outburst in the heart of Europe. Engels, who had moved to London in the summer of 1870, was accused of transforming the International into a secret society, while the *Pall-Mall Gazette* wrote that Marx had "placed himself at the head of a vast conspiracy whose objective is the realization of political Communism."[159]

James H. Billington (1929–2018), a history professor at Harvard and Princeton, documented, in a thoughtful book titled *Fire in the Mind of Men: Origins of the Revolutionary Faith*, the conspiratorial and occult origins of the principle political movements of the nineteenth and twentieth centuries, identifying in Phillipe Buonarroti the "apostle" of a conspiracy that links the French Revolution with the Communist revolutions in Eastern Europe and Asia. "Viewed from above," writes Billington, "the revolutionary tradition is the history of an élite, a tight circle of

[158] Gian Mario Bravo, *Da Weitling a Marx. La Lega dei comunisti* [*From Weitling to Marx: The Communist League*], La Pietra, Milan 1977, p. 71.

[159] E. Verdecchia, *La Londra dei cospiratori* [*The London of the Conspirators*], p. 555.

intellectual directors: a fine line of apostolic succession from Buonarroti to Lenin."[160]

The existence of this conspiratorial tradition is documented and unassailable. Among historians, Catholic and anti-Catholic, right-wing or left-wing, there can be differences in the interpretation of the facts, but not concerning their existence.

10. From the First to the Second World War

The long century that ran from the French Revolution to the First World War is the epoch in which the political and cultural inheritors of Jacobinism proposed to bring to completion the ideas of radical equality and liberty first posited by the French Revolution. This revolutionary process attained its result in the Great World War of 1914–1918, which crushed the majority of European monarchies, and in the October Revolution, which proposed to overthrow the very pillars of society, beginning with private property.

The spark that set off the First World War was a political crime: the killing of the Archduke Franz Ferdinand of Austria at the hands of Gavrilo Princip (1894–1918), on June 28, 1914. Gavrilo Princip belonged to the movement *Mlada Bosna* (Young Serbia), the political-revolutionary organization that, with the help of the secret society *Crna Ruka* (Black Hand), planned the assassination attempt. More than a restricted *congiura,* it was a widespread conspiracy upon which light has not yet been fully shed.

The Hungarian historian François Fejtö exposed the ideological aspect of the war of 1914–1918 conducted to bring to fulfillment the French Revolution. After the victory, Republican France, missionary of progress and of free thought, entrusted to peace the

[160] James H. Billington, *Fire in the Mind of Men: Origins of the Revolutionary Faith,* Basic Books, New York 1980, p. 27.

goal of "republicanizing Europe."[161] In the chapter of the book dedicated to *The Role of Freemasonry*,[162] Fejtö writes that, "it was Freemasonry, an elite organization, well structured, better organized and more centralized than political parties, that would carry out a cutting edge role in the transformation of the war of power into an ideological war for the republicanizing of Europe: a Europe grouped into a Society of Nations (an essentially Masonic idea) once the heads of the hydra of clericalism and militaristic monarchy were finally decapitated."[163] Although one cannot affirm that it was Freemasonry that overthrew the Hapsburg Empire, "it is undeniable that the fact of demolishing Austria corresponded to the ideas of the Freemasons in France and in the United States, that they were almost unreservedly in favor of its dismantling, and that their influence contributed to it."[164]

The significance of the war could have been summarized by one of Mazzini's slogans: "*Austria delenda est.*" "This doctrine," according to Fejtö, was offered to French and international Freemasonry by two geniuses of propaganda: Thomas Masaryk (1850–1937) and Edward Beneš (1884–1948), both affiliated with Freemasonry.[165] The conviction of the necessity of destroying Austria-Hungary was matured in their contacts with the most illustrious exponents of the French Grande Oriente, such as Léon Bourgeois (1851–1925) and Ernest Denis (1849–1921), who announced the creation of a cosmopolitan Society of the Nations on the ashes of the Austro-Hungarian Empire. At the end of June 1917, a conference was held at the Grand Orient in Paris, in Rue

[161] François Fejtö, *Requiem per un impero defunto. La dissoluzione del mondo austro-ungarico* [*Requiem for the Dead; The Dissolution of the Austro-Hungarian World*], tr. It. Mondadori, Milan 1990, pp. 320–21.

[162] Ibid., pp. 349–62.

[163] Ibid., p. 349.

[164] Ibid., p. 357.

[165] Ibid., p. 361.

Cadet, of all the allied and neutral Freemasons, to decide the future layout of European nations in the postwar period.[166] The basic philosophy was contained in a book by Ernest Nys (1851–1920), *Idées modernes, droit international et franc-maçonnerie*, which expounded the Masonic plan of the new international society.[167] Since the 1920s, the Polish Count Emmanuel Malynsky (1875–1938) had been analyzing in more than fifteen books the *Nouvelle Babel* of the postwar period, above all regarding Eastern and Central Europe.[168] The disappearance of the Austro-Hungarian Empire had destabilized Europe, opening the path to Communism, National Socialism, and then to the Second World War.

Everything the Bolsheviks did to acquire power in 1917 was the fruit of the conspiratorial activity of Vladimir Lenin (1870–1924) aided by the merchant Aleksander Israel Helphand (1867–1924), called Parvus. Parvus was "the only one in the world," according to Aleksandr Solzhenitsyn (1918–2008), "who could truly compete with him, and most of the time victoriously, always a step ahead of him."[169] Daniel Pipes, in his book *The Dark Side of History*,[170] describes Lenin as a conspirator who "organized his party as a tight, hierarchical structure, vowed to secrecy.... Even after having attained power, Lenin continued to think and to behave like a conspirator."[171] As the inheritor of the conspiratorial tradition of the nineteenth century, the Third International or Comintern (the international organization of Communist parties

[166] The acts of the congress were published by Léon de Poncins in *S.D.N. Super-état maçonnique*, Beauchesne, Paris 1936, pp. 63–122.

[167] Ernest Nys, *Idées modernes, droit international et franc-maçonnerie* [*Modern Ideas, International Law, and Freemasonry*], M. Weissenbruch, Bruxelles 1908.

[168] Emmanuel Malynsky, *La Nouvelle Babel* [*The New Babel*], Librarie Cervantes, Paris 1930; *Les problèmes de l'Est et la Petite Entente* [*Eastern Problems and the Little Entente*], Cervantes, Paris 1931, *et alia*.

[169] Aleksandr Solzhenitsyn, *Lenin a Zurigo* [*Lenin to Zurich*], tr. It. Mondadori, Milan 1976, p. 133.

[170] D. Pipes, *Il lato oscuro della storia* [*The Dark Side of History*], p. 335.

[171] F. Fejtö, *Requiem per un impero defunto* [*Requiem for the Dead: The Dissolution of the Austro-Hungarian World*], cit., pp. 334–35.

created by Lenin in 1919 and guided after his death by Grigory Zinoviev), constituted a powerful web integrated with diplomacy and espionage networks of the Soviet state abroad, to plan all possible actions of a revolutionary character throughout the world.

Freemasonry was not a stranger to these projects. In 1919, at the fall of Bela Kun (1886–1938), head of the Hungarian Soviet Republic, the government confiscated the Masonic archives of the Budapest lodge. After having shown the responsibility of Freemasonry in the Communist Revolution of Hungary, the new government outlawed it throughout the entire Magyar territory.[172]

The Archive of Extraordinary Ecclesiastical Affairs of the Holy See contains striking informative notes from the years 1923 and 1924, discovered through Bolshevik sources, on the expansionist plans of the Red Army in Europe and in the Middle East; these notes forecasted revolutions in Mexico and in Spain and show the vastness of the strategic design.[173]

The attempts at violent Communist revolution around the world, beginning with the so-called Red Biennium (1919–1921), provoked a strong anti-Communist reaction. Riding the wave of this reaction, fascist movements were born and consolidated. These have been perceptively defined as "anti-Bolshevik Bolshevism."[174] The historian Gonzague de Reynold (1880–1970) observed, "National Socialism was for Germany and the countries under its influence the equivalent of the French Revolution: a revolution in the German style, romantic and dynamic, but a revolution of the extreme left."[175] The great

[172] L. de Poncins, *Les forces Secrètes de la Révolution* [*The Secret Forces of Revolution*], Éditions Bossard, Paris 1928, pp. 91–98.

[173] AA. EE. SS., Russia, Pos. 626, fasc. 16, ff. 64–72.

[174] Luciano Pellicani, *La società dei giusti. Parabola storica dello gnosticismo rivoluzionario* [*The Society of the Righteous: Historical Parabola of Revolutionary Gnosticism*], Etas Libri, Milan 1995, p. 182.

[175] Gonzague de Reynold, *D'où vient l'Allemagne* [*Where Germany Comes From*], Librairie Plon, Paris 1939, pp. 222–23.

"European Civil War,"[176] conducted between Communism and National Socialism and, therefore, between the Third Reich and the Soviet Union, was the battle between two "fraternal enemies," of which the Molotov-Ribbentrop non-aggression pact, signed in Moscow on August 23, 1939, demonstrated the substantial affinity.

In his encyclical *Divini Redemptoris* of March 19, 1937, Pope Pius XI affirmed that a potent aid to the diffusion of Communism was constituted by the "conspiracy of silence" of the world press. "We say conspiracy, because otherwise one cannot explain how the press, so avid to emphasize even the most insignificant daily incidents, could have kept silent for so long about the horrors committed in Russia, in Mexico and also in much of Spain, and says relatively little about such a vast world organization such as Moscow's Communism. This silence is due in part to the reasons of a less foreseeable policy and is favored by various occult forces which for some time have sought to destroy the Christian social order."

11. Wall Street and the Revolutions of the Twentieth Century

In the seventy years running from 1917 to the fall of the Berlin Wall, the "conspiracy of silence" of which Pius XI spoke was often accompanied in the West by an international policy of complicity and support for Communism. Those who wish to deepen their knowledge of the twentieth century will benefit from reading *Tragedy and Hope*, the masterpiece of the historian Carroll Quigley (1910–1977).[177] Quigley was a professor

[176] Ernst Nolte, *Nazionalsocialismo e bolscevismo. La guerra civile europea 1917–1945* [*National Socialism and Bolshevism: The European Civil War 1917–1945*], tr. It. Sansoni, Florence 1988.

[177] Carroll Quigley, *Tragedy and Hope: A History of the World in Our Time,* The Macmillan Company, New York; Collier Macmillan, London 1966. Prof. Quigley's work was used by W. Cleon Skousen (1913–2006) in his synthesis *The Naked Capitalist* (1962).

at Georgetown University, cited by Bill Clinton in his nomination speech as a presidential candidate in 1992 as the main source of inspiration for his vocation in political life. According to Quigley, between 1860 and 1960, an Anglo-American financial network sought to dominate the world by imposing its values: "I know how this network functions, having studied it for twenty years and having been permitted to examine the documents and secret archives for two years in the 1960s. I feel no aversion to this organization, and neither for most of its goals. I have been close to it and to its instruments for most of my life. I objected, both in the past and more recently, only to some of its political views, but in general the only divergence of opinions consists in the fact that the System wants to remain anonymous, while I believe that its role is so important that it must be made known."[178]

In his book, Quigley describes how over the course of the nineteenth century some international banking families transformed into vast and secret spheres of power. "The most important of these dynasties was naturally the one formed by the descendants of Meyer Amschel Rothschild (1743–1812) of Frankfurt, whose descendants married for at least two generations either among first cousins or even among nephews. The five children of Rothschild who settled in Vienna, London, Naples, Paris, and Frankfurt collaborated among themselves in a way that was imitated, though rarely equaled, by many other international banking dynasties."[179]

These bankers, known in England as merchant bankers, in France as private bankers, and in the United States as investment bankers, developed their power above all at the tail end of the nineteenth century and the dawn of the twentieth century. The goal they aimed to reach was "nothing less than to create a world system of financial control, managed with feudal methods and placed in the

[178] Quigley, *Tragedy and Hope*, p. 950.

[179] Ibid., pp. 51–52.

hands of private individuals capable of dominating the political system of every country and the entire world economy. How could they fulfill this objective in practice? Both by means of the common action of central banks spread around the world as well as through secret agreements reached over the course of frequent private meetings and conferences."[180]

The workings of these financial dynasties had already been described by authors set aside by academic historiography like Henri Coston (1910–2001).[181] What Quigley brings to light again is the role that was carried out within this system by Cecil Rhodes[182] (1853–1902), the British diamond merchant whose name was given to the African nation Rhodesia. A recent biographer of Rhodes, Robin Brown, confirmed that he founded in 1891, with the help of the English journalist William T. Stead (1840–1912), a secret society that had as its goal "the extension of British rule throughout the world." Rhodes was succeeded by Lord Alfred Milner (1854–1925) as director of the conspiracy. Milner founded in 1909 the movement *The Round Table,* from which the Royal Institute of International Affairs of London was born.

The structure created by these magnates of Big Banking was extremely complex. In the United States, the secret society had two hubs, one in the heart of New York at the behest of the J. P. Morgan bank, the other in Ohio, led by the Rockefeller family. The New York group, Anglophile and cosmopolitan, took the name of Council on Foreign Relations, and for more than fifty years facilitated the penetration into the West of left-wing political movements with the aim of controlling them. According to Quigley, for example, the Morgan,

[180] Ibid., p. 324.

[181] See for example Henri Coston, *Les financiers qui mènent le Monde* [*The Financiers Who Run the World*], La Librairie Française, Paris 1955.

[182] Robin Brown, *The Secret Society: Cecil John Rhodes' Plan for a New World Order*, Penguin, London 2015.

Rockefeller, and Carnegie foundations, through the Institute of Pacific Relations, pushed China into the international Communist block after World War Two.[183]

Quigley ignores the role of Freemasonry, despite it being known that they were affiliated with some of the protagonists of his book, beginning with Rhodes, a member of the Apollo University Lodge of Oxford and the *Ars Quatuor Coronatorum* of London, the first lodge in the world dedicated to Masonic studies.[184] On the other hand, Jessica Harland-Jacobs, in her book *Builders of Empire: Freemasons and British Imperialism*, amply documented the role of Freemasonry in the diffusion of British imperialism.[185] Furthermore, Quigley's work, despite its bulk of nearly 1,300 pages, fails to cite a single note or document in support of his affirmations.

In this regard the American historian Anthony C. Sutton (1925–2002) seems a more reliable source. On the basis of nearly totally original documentation, contents from the American National Archives, he demonstrated the existence of economic assistance on the part of the financiers of Wall Street for revolutions *and* for political movements apparently opposed to them such as the Bolshevik Revolution of 1917, National Socialism, and Roosevelt's New Deal.[186] If one were to trace these surprising connections to a game of pure economic interests, one's conclusions would be limited to a secondary aspect of historical reality, a reality that is moved by the ideas and tendencies of the human soul, which are more profound than material interests.

[183] Quigley, *Tragedy and Hope*, pp. 946–47.

[184] Joe Mordaunt Crook, James W. Daniel, *Oxford Freemasons: A Social History of the Apollo University Lodge*, Bodleian Library, Oxford 2018.

[185] Jessica Harland-Jacobs, *Builders of Empire: Freemasons and British Imperialism, 1717–1927*, The University of North Carolina Press, Chapel Hill 2007.

[186] Anthony C. Sutton, *Wall Street and the Bolshevik Revolution*, Arlington House, New York 1974; *Wall Street and Franklin Delano Roosevelt*, Arlington House, New York 1975; *Wall Street and the Rise of Hitler*, '76 Press, Seal Beach 1976.

12. Synarchism and Modernism

The coexistence of economic and religious perspectives in the same people and in the same movements is visible in the figure of Count Claude-Henry de Saint-Simon (1760–1825), who theorized the reform of European society according to the model of a large corporation in which political power over people would be transformed into the science of production and of the administration of goods. This social transformation ought to have been favored by the humanitarian religion of the "New Christianity" announced by him. His followers founded therefore the new religion of "Saint-Simonism," of which Prosper Enfantin (1796–1864) was the "pontiff".

Alexandre Saint-Yves d'Alveydre (1842–1909), a French occultist of the nineteenth century, believed as did the Saint-Simonians in the indefinite progress of humanity thanks to "science," which for him, however, is "occult" science learned from the ancient Egyptians and in the Far East. Saint-Yves developed the idea of the Synarchy, a project of societal reform structured through political, economic, and spiritual power. Saint-Yves was also convinced of the existence of a super-government of humanity situated in a legendary subterranean kingdom called Agartha, which he supposedly learned of during his travels in India.

The work of Saint-Yves was known only by a small number of adherents, until June 1941, when the prefect Henry Chavin, the director of Sûreté Nationale under the regime of Marshal Philippe Pétain (1940–1944), published a report in which he accused the engineer Jean Coutrot (1895–1941) of having founded a secret society called MSE (*Mouvement synachique d'empire*), with the aim of reorganizing society after the Second World War.

Henry Coston published the *Pacte synarchiste révolutionnaire pour l'Empire français* of this group of technocrats,[187] while Louis

[187] H. Coston, *Les technocrats et la Synarchie* [*Technocrats and Synarchy*], La Librairie Française, Paris 1979, pp. 115–94.

Daménie (1912–1972) analyzed their doctrine, demonstrating that it was a version of the philosophy of Saint-Yves, addressing the high functionaries of administration and finance.[188]

The Catholic writer Pierre Virion (1889–1988), in his *Mystère d'iniquité,* described the penetration of synarchic ideas within the Catholic Church, thanks to the work of *Abbé* Paul Roca (1830–1893), an apostate priest of Perpignan, disciple of Saint-Yves d'Alveydre.[189] Roca was the author of a work titled *Les Nouveaux Cieux et la Nouvelle Terre* (1886), placed on the Church's Index of Prohibited Books, in which he proclaimed that "the new social order will be inaugurated outside of Rome, without Rome, despite Rome, against Rome."[190] These expressions remind us of those conspirators of the Alta Vendita and of the initiated *Eques a Capite Galeato,* who in his notes wrote of Rome in this manner: "Haughty and proud city that dominated from one pole to the other, that gave laws to the entire universe, what has happened to your power? What did your triumphs win you? The memory of your glory was preserved; your name exists still; but that is all, and you are no more."[191]

The work of Pierre Teilhard de Chardin (1881–1955) resonates with that of Saint-Yves d'Alveydre and the *Abbé* Roca. To the historical Christ of the Gospel, Teilhard de Chardin opposed a cosmic Christ who identifies with the evolution of the universe. According to Plinio Corrêa de Oliveira, in his cosmic evolutionism, Teilhard overturned

[188] Louis Daménie, *La technocratie carrefour de la subversion* [*Technocracy: The Crossroads of Subversion*], Dominique Martin Morin, Bouère 1988.

[189] Pierre Virion, *Mystère d'iniquité* [*Mystery of Iniquity*], Éditions Saint-Michel, Saint-Céneré 1967.

[190] Cit. in Marie-France James, *Esotérisme, occultisme, franc-maçonnerie et christianisme aux XIXe et XXe siècles. Explorations bio-bibliographiques* [*Esotericism, Occultism, Freemasonry, and Christianity in the Nineteenth and Twentieth Centuries: Bio-bibliographical Explorations*], Nouvelles Éditions Latines, Paris 1981, p. 230.

[191] B. Fabre, *Franciscus, Eques a Capite Galeato*, p. 130.

the Gnostic thesis of the descent by means of emanation, from the spirit to matter, to imagine an ascent by means of evolution, from matter to the spirit, understood as "the superior state of matter."[192]

Evolutionism and pantheism characterized theological modernism, the philosophical-religious current proposed to reconcile Christianity with the modern world. Modernism was condemned on September 8, 1907, by St. Pius X (r. 1903–1914) in his encyclical *Pascendi*.[193] Three years later, in his motu proprio *Sacrorum Antistitum* of September 1, 1910, the pope advanced the hypothesis that modernism had a unitary subterranean organization, going so far as to form a downright "secret society" within the Church. Modernists, in fact, wrote St. Pius X, "have never ceased to search and to create a secret association of new proselytes and, by means of them, to inject into the veins of Christian society the poison of their opinions using the publication of books and pamphlets without divulging the names of their authors."[194]

Fr. Gioacchino Ambrosini (1857–1923) shed light on the analogy between the modernist novel *The Saint* by Antonio Fogazzaro (1842–1911) and the ideas of Theosophy in a book which appeared in 1907 on the theme *The Occult and Modernism*.[195] In Fogazzaro's novel, he describes a religious sect that meets secretly in Subiaco to elaborate a "faith purified for adults" fit for reforming Christianity. According to

[192] Cf. R. de Mattei, *Plinio Corrêa de Oliveira, Apostolo di Fatima, Profeta del Regno di Maria* [*Plinio Corrêa de Oliveira, Apostle of Fatima, Prophet of the Kingdom of Mary*], Edizioni Fiducia, Rome 2017, pp. 90–91.

[193] S. Pio X, Enciclica *Pascendi Dominici gregis* of September 8, 1907, in AAS, vol. 40 (1907), pp. 596–628.

[194] Ibid.

[195] Gioacchino Ambrosini, *Occultismo e modernismo. Lettere familiari ad un amico* [*The Occult and Modernism: Family Letters to a Friend*], Tipografia Arcivescovile, Bologna 1907, on which cf. Adele Cerreta, *Le origini esoteriche del modernismo. Padre Gioacchino Ambrosini e la teologia modernista* [*The Esoteric Origins of Modernism: Fr. Gioacchino Ambrosini and Modernist Theology*], Solfanelli, Chieti 2012.

Fr. Ambrosini, this religious reform is nothing more than the doctrine of Theosophy, of which Fogazzaro was an adherent.

In 1910, the *Abbé* Emmanuel Barbier (1851–1925) published *Les infiltrations maçonniques dans l'Église,* in which he described the penetration of esotericism into Catholic settings, above all following the Masonic Spiritualist Convention held in Paris in 1908, at the initiative of the Martinist lodges.[196] The founder of the Martinist Order, the "magician" and fortune teller Gérard Encausse (1865–1916), known by the pseudonym of "Papus," inaugurated the convention, whose secretary was René Guénon (1886–1951), exponent of the "Gnostic Church," founded by Jules Doinel (1842–1902).[197] The spiritualist conference had the goal of creating, under the pretext of reacting against materialism, a federation of different Gnostic, Theosophic, and cabalistic sects, as well as undertaking a restoration of Freemasonry, deteriorated and discredited after its politicization in France.[198] "Spiritualist" Freemasonry performed another role as well, however: namely, to corrupt Catholic environments where an effective anti-Masonic reaction was being organized. From September 26 to September 30, 1816, an important anti-Masonic convention took place in Trent organized by a committee presided by the attorney Guglielmo Alliata (1852–1937), founder of the Anti-Masonic Union in Rome. During an extraordinary session of the convention, presided by the vice president of the Anti-Masonic Union, Pietro Pacelli (1831–1904), the uncle of future Pope Pius XII, Alliata

[196] Emmanuel Barbier, *Les infiltrations maçonniques dans l'Église [Masonic Infiltration of the Church],* Société Saint-Augustin, Paris 1910, pp. 103–112.

[197] M. James, *Esotérisme, occultisme, franc-maçonnerie et christianisme* [*Esotericism, Occultism, Freemasonry, and Christianity*], p. 103. On Doinel, see M. Introvigne, *Il ritorno dello gnosticismo* [*The Return of Gnosticism*], Sugarco, Milan 1993, pp. 96–125.

[198] Ibid., p. 145–46.

publicly exposed the presumed revelations of Léo Taxil, who was present at the session.[199]

In 1885, Gabriel Antoine Jogand-Pagès (1854–1907) feigned his conversion to Freemasonry and, under the pseudonym of Leo Taxil, made a series of sensational revelations about satanism being practiced in the Masonic lodges. In 1897, however, after the conference in Trent, he declared during a public meeting that he had invented everything to mock Catholics and returned to his previous anticlericalism, dying an unrepentant freethinker. Msgr. Antonino Romeo (1902–1979), one of the most reliable scholars of satanism, held that this hoaxer invented only the sensational and picturesque details, while the substance of Masonic satanism had been denounced by many authors long before Taxil.[200]

More sophisticated than that of Taxil was the role of "corruptor" played by René Guénon in Catholic circles after the Masonic conference of 1908. In 1913, for example, when a debate in Catholic periodicals began on the theme of the "Incognito Superiors" of Freemasonry, Guénon fueled a virulent polemic with his interventions under a pseudonym, in the magazine *La France chrétienne Antimaçonnique.*[201] René Guénon, at that moment, was a bishop in the Gnostic Church under the name Palingenius; later he would be initiated into Sufi Islam under the name of Sheik Abd al-Wahid Yahya, Freemason of the Thébah lodge and "prince occultist." This did not

[199] *Actes du 1er Congrès Antimaçonnique international* [*Proceedings of the First International Anti-Masonic Congress*], 2 vol., Desclée, Tournai 1897, p. xiv. Thirty-six bishops, five hundred episcopal delegates, and seven hundred delegates from Catholic organizations around the world took part at the conference.

[200] Msgr. A. Romeo, *Satanismo* [*Satanism*], in *Enciclopedia Cattolica*, vol. 10 (1953), col. 1958 (col. 1953–1961).

[201] See "La polémique sur les 'Supérieurs inconnus'" [The Unknown Superiors Controversy], in *Charis. Archives de l'Unicorne*, Arché, Milan 2003; Michel Jarrige, *L'antimaçonnerie en France à la Belle Epoque* [*Anti-Masonry in France During the Belle Epoque*], Arché, Milan 2004, pp. 686–89.

prevent him from collaborating in Catholic periodicals, such as *Revue Philosophique* and *Regnabit,* until in 1930 he left for Cairo, where he died an observant Muslim.

13. Revolution and Satanism

We might ask the question at this point: considering the existence of a variety of secret societies and occult forces that run throughout history, is it possible to speak of one great conspiracy to which the individual plots and conspiracies, or at least some of them, can be attributed?

To admit the hypothesis of a universal conspiracy in history, one needs to postulate the existence of an enemy, likewise universal and perennial as the target of conspirators. Under this aspect, the only subject on offer as the object of a universal conspiracy is the Catholic Church, insofar as it is a perennial institution, founded by Jesus Christ, and destined to guide history until the end of times. There is no other conspiracy possible besides an antichristian conspiracy, which, as such, has often been denounced by popes in their Magisterium.

In the encyclical *Mirari vos* of August 15, 1832, Gregory XVI denounced the "conspiracy of the blasphemous" that causes "the undermining of public order, the decline of principalities and the undoing of every legitimate power," affirming that "a heap of misadventures this enormous must be attributable in particular to the conspiracy of those societies in which it seems there are gathered, as if in a lurid den, all that is sacrilegious, abominable and impious in the heresies and most wicked sects."[202]

His successors, Pius IX (1846–1878) and Leo XIII (1878–1903), often repeat this concept. In one of the last documents of his pontificate, the encyclical *Annum ingressi* of March 19, 1902, Leo XIII described the history of the fight and triumph of the Church

[202] Gregorio XVI, Enc. *Mirari vos* of August 15, 1832, in *Acta Gregorii XVI,* vol. I (1901), p. 169.

with the intention of "considering in its genesis, in its causes, in its various forms, the war that rages to the harm of the Church."[203]

The existence of an "enemy" that conspires against the Church and Christian society is repeated by Pius XII (1939–1958), who claimed this enemy was everywhere and in the midst of all things, and is capable of being violent or subtle as the occasion demands. "In these past few centuries, [this enemy] has attempted to work through the intellectual, moral, and social disintegration of the unity of the mysterious organism of Christ. It has desired nature without grace; reason without faith; liberty without authority; at times authority without liberty. It is an 'enemy' evermore concrete, with an irreverence that still leaves one speechless: *Christ yes, Church no,* then: *God yes, Christ no*. Finally, it shouts blasphemously: *God is dead; no: God never existed*. And behold the attempt to build the structure of the world on the foundations that we do not hesitate to declare as the principal bearer of responsibility for the threat that looms over humanity: an economy without God, politics without God."[204]

The processes enduring for centuries that place in opposition the antichristian revolution against the Catholic Church, the one Teacher and Source of life for the nations, was masterfully described by Plinio Corrêa de Oliveira in his work *Revolution and Counter-Revolution*. The Brazilian professor affirms the existence of a chain of intellectual errors that developed down the centuries. He claims, however, that the great modifications in the spirit of peoples have their origin in the deeper tendencies of the human soul. The dynamism of disordered passions and of human errors is not sufficient to explain the revolutionary process. One principle of *Revolution and Counter-Revolution* affirms that all forms of evil end up being connected, even when they were not

[203] Leone XIII, Enc. *Annum ingressi* of March 19, 1902, in *Enchiridion, Leone XIII*, p. 1895 (pp. 1892–931).

[204] Pio XII, *Nel contemplare,* discourse to the men of Catholic Action of October 12, 1952, in *Discourses and Radio Messages,* vol. XIV, p. 359.

concocted by one person or by the same center. To direct a revolutionary process, chaotic as such, the impulse and direction of knowledgeable agents are necessary. "To produce a process as cohesive and continuous as that of revolution, through thousands of vicissitudes of entire centuries, full of all types of unforeseen events, seems impossible without the action of successive generations of conspirators possessed by extraordinary intelligence and power."[205]

All of the secret sects and forces that propose as their goal the destruction of the Church and Christian civilization can and should be considered agents of revolution. The identity of the conspirators can vary, but, in light of Catholic theology, the permanent director of the revolutionary process is Satan, the fallen angel, always in rebellion and always defeated. The history of secret societies and their conspiracies is assumed into the great framework of the battle between the Two Cities, the City of God and the City of Satan, summarized thus by St. Augustine: "The former is the society of devout men, the latter of rebels, each with the angels belonging to them, in which on one side the love of God reigns supreme, and on the other the love of self."[206]

The existence of a City of Satan opposed to the City of God, which is the Church, postulates the existence of a "counter-church" and an explicit or implicit demonolatry. Fr. Paolo Siano dedicated in-depth studies on Masonic Luciferianism, confuting the theses of those who hold that this would be cultivated only by a "fringe Freemasonry," marginal and thus extraneous to regular Freemasonry.[207] General Albert Pike (1809–1891), director of the Ancient and Accepted Scottish

[205] P. Corrêa de Oliveira, *Rivoluzione e Contro-Rivoluzione* [*Revolution and Counter-Revolution*], p. 90.

[206] St. Augustine, *The City of God*, lib. XIV, c. 13, 1.

[207] Paolo M. Siano, *La Massoneria tra esoterismo, ritualità e simbolismo* [*Freemasonry, Esoterism, Rituality and Symbolism*], vol. I, *Studi vari sulla Libera Muratoria*, Casa Mariana Editrice, Frigento (var. authors) 2012, pp. 195–284, 477–529.

Rite of Freemasonry, writes in his book *Morals and Dogma* (1871), defined by the *Encyclopédie de la Franc-Maçonnerie* as a Masonic "masterpiece,"[208] that the initiatory itinerary of the Freemason consists in descending into Hell and accepting the exact contrary of Catholic dogma to ascend to the light, "using the devil as a monstrous ladder."[209]

With the support of Pike, Adriano Lemmi (1822–1906), Grand Master of Italian Freemasonry in the years 1885–1889, reunited the Grand Orient with the Ancient and Accepted Scottish Rite. Under his governance, in 1893, Freemasonry rented the nobility quarters of the Palazzo Borghese in Rome. The new headquarters was opened on September 20, and from that morning the green flag of Freemasonry was exposed from the balcony. In the Hall of the Thirty-Three, in the presence of more than two hundred Masonic delegates from around the world, Grand Master Lemmi expressed his satisfaction at being able to preside over the opening of the new temple in the palace whose owners belonged to a religion they sought to crush.

Two years later, Prince Scipione Borghese (1871–1927), on the occasion of his marriage to Duchess Anna Maria De Ferrari, requested that the premises be returned to his possession. When the head of the affairs of the Borghese family arrived to visit those apartments, one of the halls remained closed and could not be opened without threatening to invoke the public authorities. According to the description given by the newspapers of the day, the walls had been covered with red and black damask and on the back wall there was a large tapestry on which the figure of Lucifer appeared. The hall

208 *Encyclopédie de la Franc-Maçonnerie* [*Encyclopedia of Freemasonry*], ed. by Eric Saunier, Librairie Générale Française, Paris 2000, p. 665.

209 P. M. Siano, *La Massoneria tra esoterismo, ritualità e simbolismo* [*Freemasonry, Esoterism, Rituality and Symbolism*], pp. 523–24.

had been transformed into a satanic temple. In the middle of this temple something resembling a throne had been placed.[210]

14. Freemasonry and Gnosis

Divine Providence is the final explanation of all that happens in the universe. Nevertheless, as writes Fr. Joseph Lémann (1836–1915), whoever considers only Providence, without taking Hell into account, can offer only an incomplete version of history. "God and Satan compete over the heart of man, we all know: but they also compete over the direction of society."[211] The Catholic historian and philosopher who studies the work of secret societies cannot ignore the diabolic dimension of the revolutionary process. A history "in which one insists on wanting to explain evil only in terms of perversity and human passions," affirms Dom Guéranger, "is neither a Christian history nor a complete history."[212]

The *civitas diaboli* is not merely a composite of errors or moral perversions, but has its own organized structure. It has dogmas, rites, and hierarchies, because it constitutes a counterfeit of the true Church; hence the book of Revelation (2:9; 3:9) defines it as the "synagogue of Satan." Tertullian describes the rituals used in the second century, revealing that already in that period a diabolical parody of Christian mysteries existed. St. Irenaeus of Lyon (130–202), the first to write against the Gnostics, speaks of the Cainites who exalted as liberators the great rebels against God: Cain, Esau, the Sodomites, and Judas.[213] The medieval heretical sects, such as the Cathars, considered as their precursors Cain, the builders of the Tower of Babel,

210 Msgr. Henri Delassus, *Il problema dell'ora presente* [*The Problem of the Present Hour*], tr. It. Desclée, Rome 1907, vol. I, p. 486.

211 Joseph Lémann, *L'entrée des Israelites dans la société française* [*Israelites' Entry into French Society*], Éditions Avalon, Paris 1987, p. 206.

212 Dom P. Guéranger, *Il senso della storia* [*The Meaning of History*], p. 76.

213 S. Ireneo di Lione, *Adversus haereses*,1, 31; PG 7,704.

and the inhabitants of the city of Sodom. But also in the founding document of Freemasonry, however, "it seems precisely that Anderson wants to underline that Cain is *the first* to have exercised, in a productive manner, the geometric bricklayers art, and thus Cain was the first effective *bricklayer* or *mason*."[214]

The studies of Jean-Claude Lozac'hmeur on the occult origins of Freemasonry show that it inherited faith and customs from Gnosticism.[215] Gnosis is a form of initiatory knowledge that, through variable expressions, runs the length of over two thousand years of history, from antiquity to our own time. In his *Church Histories*, the first historian of the Church, Eusebius of Caesarea (265–340), like the Fathers of the Church before him, dates the origins of Gnosis to Simon Magus, who the Acts of the Apostles says seduced the people of Samaria "saying that he himself was somebody great. They all gave heed to him, from the least to the greatest" (Acts 8:9–10).

The common principle to all the Gnostic sects is the idea of an instruction reserved to a few initiates, preserved from antiquity and betrayed by the Catholic Church. Gnosis presents itself, therefore, as a technique of knowledge, thanks to which man enters into possession of the keys of the cosmic mystery and "recognizes" his own divine nature, abolishing his individuality in the unconscious Absolute. In this respect, it is a mysticism, albeit upside down with respect to Christianity.

An initiatory link seems to connect those who, from the beginning of humanity to the present day, pass on these occultist theses. According to the British theologian Ronald H. Knox (1888–1957), there exists "a subterranean world of heresy which secretly undermined the

[214] P. M. Miano, *La Massoneria tra esoterismo, ritualità e simbolismo* [*Freemasonry Between Esotericism, Ritual, and Symbolism*], vol. I, p. 52.

[215] Jean-Claude Lozac'hmeur, *Fils de la veuve: essai sur le symbolisme maçonnique* [*Son of the Widow: Essay on Masonic Symbolism*], Éditions Sainte Jeanne d'Arc, Chiré-en-Montreuil 1990.

structure of medieval Europe."[216] This "subterranean river," from its medieval wellsprings, flows toward the estuary of Deism and the Enlightenment and from there drains into the antichristian ideologies of the last two centuries. Many scholars, such as Igor Safarevic (1923–2017), have demonstrated the genetic links that connect the ancient and medieval heresies, Protestant sects, the French Revolution, and the socialist movements of the nineteenth and twentieth centuries.[217]

According to the Magisterium of the Church, the mother sect, "permanent personification of revolution," around which all the others are organized as simple auxiliary forces, (at times knowingly, at other time unknowingly) is Freemasonry, as is revealed clearly from the pontifical documents that have repeatedly condemned it over the centuries.[218]

15. The Church and Freemasonry

The first papal condemnation of Freemasonry dates to the apostolic letter *In eminenti* of Clement XII from April 28, 1738, which ordered the bishops to proceed against Masons as persons suspected *vehementer* of heresy. From then onward, the condemnations followed uninterrupted.[219] The excommunication was confirmed and renewed by Benedict XIV with the constitution *Provida* of May 18, 1751, and from Pius VII with the constitution *Ecclesiam a Jesu Christo* of September 13, 1821.

216 Ronald A. Knox, *Enthusiasm: A Chapter in the History of Religion*, University of Notre Dame Press, Notre Dame 1994 (1950).

217 Igor Safarevic, *Il socialismo come fenomeno storico mondiale* [*Socialism as a Global Historical Phenomenon*], tr. It. La Casa di Matriona, Milan 1980.

218 Leo XIII, Enc. *Annum ingressi*, p. 1919.

219 The acts concerning Freemasonry issued from the Holy See up until 1917 can be found complete and in chronological order in *Codici iuris canonici fontes* ed. Em. P. Card. Gasparri (Libreria Editrice Vaticana, Rome 1929–1939, 9 vol.): vol. II, nn. 412, 479, 481, 504, 507, 508, 542, 544; vol. III, nn. 552, 563, 571, 591; vol. IV, nn. 877, 869, 899, 932, 1012, 1036, 1080, 1085, 1100, 1204; vol. VII, nn. 4871, 4910, 4937; vol. VIII, n. 6432.

On March 13, 1825, the apostolic constitution *Quo graviora* of Leo XII repeated the previous censures, clarifying that these applied to every secret society, present or future, whatever its name, that had as its aim to conspire to the detriment of the Church and of the powers of the states. Expressing the same line were Pius VIII with the encyclical *Traditi humiliate* of May 24, 1829, Gregory XVI with the encyclical *Mirari vos* of August 15, 1832, Pius IX with the encyclical *Qui pluribus* of November 9, 1846, the Constitution *Apostolicae Sedis* of October 12, 1869, and many other interventions.

In his encyclical *Humanum genus* of April 20, 1884, Leo XIII denounced the diabolical plot of Freemasonry which, the pope affirmed, has as its "final and main intention that of destroying from top to bottom the entire religious and social order as it was created by Christianity, and taking foundations and norms from naturalism, entirely remaking it to their liking."[220]

The same Leo XIII, in the apostolic letter *Annum ingressi* of March 19, 1902, reviewed the stages throughout the centuries of the war waged against the Church by antichristian forces. He dwelt on the role carried out by "a dark sect which society has carried for many years in its bowels, like a mortal disease, which contaminates sanctity, fecundity, and life. It constitutes a type of inverted society, whose aim is the occult predominance over recognized society and whose reason for existing consists in war against God and His Church. It would not even be necessary to name it because all carry this one mark, Freemasonry, of which we spoke in our encyclical *Humanum genus* of April 20, 1884, denouncing its evil tendencies, its false doctrines, its nefarious works. This sect which embraces in its immense dragnet nearly every nation and is linked with other sects that move with hidden strings enticing its affiliates with the bait of

[220] Leo XIII, Enc. *Humanum genus* of April 20, 1884, in *Enchiridion, Leone XIII*, p. 295 (pp. 286–321).

advantages they can procure, bending governors to their designs first with promises and then with threats, has reached a level of infiltration into all social strata, and forms almost an invisible, irresponsible state within the legitimate state. Full of the spirit of Satan who, as the Apostle said, knows how to transform himself into an angel of light when needed (2 Cor. 11:14), boasts of humanitarian objectives, but exploits everything with its sectarian purpose, and while declaring to have no political aims, it exercises broad action in legislative and administrative movements of the state, while it professes respect for reigning authorities and even for religion, its supreme aim (and its own regulations affirm it) is the extermination of the empire and the priesthood, considered by them enemies of freedom."[221]

The condemnation of Freemasonry was included in canons 684, 2335, and 2336 of the Code of Canon Law in force from 1917 to 1983. Canon 2335 of the old Code provided for the excommunication of "all those who join the Masonic sect or other associations of the same type, which plot against the Church and against legitimate civil powers."

With the new Code of Canon Law, excommunication with respect to Freemasonry is not explicitly cited, although article 1374 reads, "A person who joins an association which plots against the Church is to be punished with a just penalty; one who promotes or takes office in such an association is to be punished with an interdict."

The Congregation for the Doctrine of the Faith, presided over by then-Cardinal Joseph Ratzinger, when asked if the judgment of the Church with respect to Freemasonry had changed due to the fact that it was not expressly mentioned in the new Code of Canon Law,

[221] Gregory XVI, Enc. *Mirari vos* of August 15, 1832, in Ugo Bellocchi, *Tutte le encicliche e i documenti pontifici*, vol. III, Libreria Editrice Vaticana, Vatican City 1994, p. 171 (pp. 169–78).

reaffirmed in the declaration *Quaesitum est* of November 26, 1983, that "the negative judgment of the Church remains unaltered as concerns Masonic associations, because their principles have always been considered incompatible with the doctrine of the Church and thus joining them remains prohibited. The faithful who belong to Masonic associations are in a state of grave sin and cannot receive Holy Communion."

This remains the position of the Church with regard to all the Masonic obediences and rites. One must always keep in mind that there corresponds to the ways of holiness toward God, Most Perfect Being and Highest Good, a multiplicity of pathways of evil that plummet into the abyss, and that Freemasonry gathers the inheritance of the ancient heresies and secret societies. For this reason, Pope Gregory XVI attributed the heap of evils that afflicted the Church "to the conspiring of those societies in which there seems to be gathered, as in a filthy den, all that is sacrilegious, abominable and blasphemous in the most wicked heresies and sects."

CHAPTER THREE

True and False Plots

1. Conspiracies and Plots

The word *plot* is often used as a synonym of *congiura* or *conspiracy*. Unlike these two terms, however, *plot* can also indicate the narrative development of a written or performed work. Plotting seems to indicate the psychological disposition of funneling all of reality into a fictitious plot. The reduction of every aspect of reality to a plot defeats in fact the reality of plots, rendering them a fiction. If all reality is a plot, no plot can be real.

Naturally, no one is so foolish as to negate the existence of plots, but the problem is that of distinguishing true plots from an imaginary "plot theory." To this end, when plots are true, it is better to substitute this term, which generates so much misunderstanding, with *conspiracy*, or *congiura*, keeping this word *plot* for the meaning of a false *congiura* or conspiracy.

The term *conspiracy theory* indicates a fictional conspiracy, but *plot theory* seems more precise to indicate a fiction. Conspiracy is real and is the object of historical study. Plots substitute reality with narration. The plot theory is therefore a narration devoid of foundations in reality. If, in the modern era, Descartes made reality depend on thought, the plotters of the postmodern era make reality depend on the imagination.

2. The *Monita Secreta* and the Popish Plot

The prototype of all plots without any basis in reality is that attributed ever since the end of the seventeenth century to the Jesuits. This occurred on the basis of an apocryphal document, the *Monita privata Societatis Jesu,* printed in Krakow around 1615 and then disseminated in hundreds of editions in every country for four centuries under the name of *Monita Secreta.*[222] The *Monita* contained the presumed Secret Instructions of the Society of Jesus, and was a forgery whose author was discovered, after an investigation by the bishop of Krakow, to be an ex-Jesuit by the name of Hieronim Zahorowski, who had accumulated hate and rancor toward the Society from which he had been expelled. The enemies of the Society of Jesus and of the Church based their attack for centuries on this forgery that attributed to the Jesuits a hidden morality, with secret rules and instructions in opposition to the declared ones to deceive the simple.

On the same lines of imaginary plots is to be found the Popish Plot, a fictitious Jesuit conspiracy to assassinate King Charles II of England (r. 1660–1685), but in reality, was invented by the Protestant fanatic Titus Oates (1649–1705) to win favor with the sovereign. The accusations, later revealed to be false, caused the death of many innocent people from 1678 to 1681, among them Oliver Plunkett, the last Catholic martyr in England, drawn and quartered in London in 1681.[223] Oates was condemned to life in prison and

222 Sabina Pavone, *Le astuzie dei gesuiti. Le false istruzioni segrete della Compagnia di Gesù e la polemica antigesuitica nei secoli XVII e XVIII* [*The Wiles of the Jesuits: The False Secret Instructions of the Society of Jesus and the Anti-Jesuit Controversy in the Seventeenth and Eighteenth Centuries*], Salerno Editrice, Rome 2000.

223 John Pollock, *The Popish Plot: A Study in the History of the Reign of Charles II,* Duckworth, London 1903; John Kenyon, *The Popish Plot,* Phoenix Press, New Haven 1985.

placed in the stocks one day each year, but after several years was given his freedom and died in obscurity.

The Jesuit plot theory was a downright ideological war machine against the Church, especially in the eighteenth and nineteenth centuries. In the eighteenth century, on the basis of these calumnies taken up again by Illuminists and Jansenists, the Society of Jesus was expelled from the Kingdoms of the House of Bourbon and suppressed by Pope Clement XIV in 1773. In the nineteenth century, the Jesuit plot became a genre of literature, as seen in the novels of Eugène Sue (1804–1857) or Alexandre Dumas (1802–1870). In *The Count of Bragelonne,* the last great novel of the trilogy of the *Three Musketeers,* a presumed general of the Jesuits entrusts on his death bed to Aramis the musketeer-turned-bishop a ring, "sign of omnipotence," which will grant him the right to life and to death, either within or outside of the order.[224]

Vincenzo Gioberti (1801–1852) collected in the five volumes of the *Modern Jesuit* (1846–47) all the most defamatory accusations against the Society of Jesus. The history of anti-Jesuit literature demonstrates how a fictional "plot theory" can be the fruit of a real conspiracy against the truth and is perpetuated with consequences at times dramatic, as in the death sentence of the Jesuit Fr. Gabriele Malagrida (1689–1761), burned in the city square with thirty-two other people in Lisbon in 1761 under the accusation of heresy and *congiura* against King Joseph of Portugal.

The center for the diffusion of anti-Jesuit activity was Freemasonry, which did not forgive the Society of Jesus for counting among their numbers some of their most formidable adversaries. It was precisely inside the occult Freemasons that there developed in the

[224] Alexandre Dumas, *Il visconte di Bragelonne* [*The Count of Bragelonne*], tr. It. Newton Compton, Rome 2016, pp. 602–13.

last thirty years of the nineteenth century a culture of "plotting" destined to sweep through the subculture of the twenty-first century.

3. From Freemasonry to Theosophy

In the second half of the nineteenth century, Freemasonry, which had its propulsive center in the French Grand Orient, offered both the managerial class and the ideology to the Third Republic which was born after the Commune of Paris in 1870. The Masonic historian Alec Mellor (1907–1988) writes, "In that moment a strange epoch of history opened, which would not end with the First World War. For nearly forty years, the Grand Orient became the real government of France, behind the mask of the official government of the nation. The anti-Masonic coalitions will mistakenly call this regime a hidden dictatorship, because it was not hidden except to those who did not wish to see it."[225]

From 1865 on, much discussion was given within the Grand Orient to the meaning of the reference to the "Grand Architect of the Universe." The Grand Master Frédéric Desmons (1832–1910), in a discourse given to the Supreme Council on September 13, 1877, approved a new Masonic constitution in which the obligation of faith in God was suppressed. The substitution of declared atheism for the generic spiritualism professed up to that moment provoked a rupture between the Grand Orient and English Freemasonry, which was still "spiritualist."

While Latin Freemasonry, which we can define as "left-wing," professed the cult of science and of reason, the pseudo-mystic "right-wing" Freemasonry of England and Germany placed in discussion

225 Alec Mellor, *La vie quotidienne de la Franc-maçonnerie française du XVIIIème siècle à nos jours* [*Daily Life in French Freemasonry from the Eighteenth Century to the Present Day*], Hachette, Paris 1973, p. 143.

esoteric doctrines that blended with the vitalism and irrationalism of the late century.

The Theosophical Society was founded in 1875 by Hélène Blavatsky (1831–1891), a swashbuckler from Russia who affirmed she had been "initiated" by "masters" who lived in an inaccessible region of Tibet. According to the secret doctrine transmitted by Blavatsky, a vital force runs through the cosmos that escapes scientific analysis, but which can be identified by soothsayers and shamans through techniques that develop the occult powers latent in man. The Theosophic doctrines harmonized with the spiritism founded in the mid-nineteenth century by Allan Kardec (pseudonym of Hippolyte Rivail: 1804–1869).

Spiritism has been known since antiquity as necromancy, a magical practice seeking to enter into contact with the kingdom of the dead. Necromantic experiments were part of the "High Magic" of Eliphas Levi (pseudonym of Alphonse-Louis Constant: 1810–1875), who claimed to have received his hidden knowledge from the spirit of Apollonius of Tyana, during an evocation that took place in London on July 24, 1854. For the Church, however, as Cardinal Alessio Lepicier (1863–1936) reminds us, "spiritualistic manifestations can be attributed neither to God, nor to the action of good angels, nor to that of the souls of the deceased, whether saved or damned. They must be attributed, therefore, to the action of the fallen angels."[226]

In London, and later in Paris, magicians, Theosophists, and spiritists frequented the salons of the clairvoyant Lady Caithness, or

[226] Alessio Maria Lepicier, *Il mondo invisibile. Esposizione della teologia cattolica intorno allo spiritismo moderno [The Invisible World: Exposition of Catholic Theology Around Modern Spiritualism]*, Società Cattolici Vicentini, Vicenza 1920, p. 186. See also Roger Gougenot des Mousseaux, *Moeurs et pratiques des démons et des esprits visiteurs du spiritisme ancien et moderne* [*Habits and Practices of Demons and Spirit Visitors to Ancient and Modern Spiritualism*], Henri Plon, Paris 1865.

Maria de Mariategui (1830–1893), Duchess of Pomar. Lady Caithness claimed to have frequent meetings with the ghost of Mary Stuart Queen of Scots and to have received from the "superior spirits" the mission of announcing to humanity the "Fourth Revelation," after that of Moses, Jesus Christ, and that of the spiritists. The goal of this revelation was the establishment of a universal religion that would replace Catholicism.

According to Theosophy, all religions derive from a single divine truth, or from a "primordial tradition," and the specific norms, institutions, and rites of religious confessions are nothing but frill. In this spirit, on September 8, 1893, the Parliament of Religions was inaugurated in Chicago, an ecumenical assembly that saw the encounter of Catholic priests, Protestant pastors, Orthodox patriarchs, Muslim muftis, Buddhist monks, and representatives of every religion, cult, and sect, to celebrate the role of inter-religious collaboration in modern society. The representatives of Theosophy and those of the "Americanist" movement of Fr. Thomas Isaac Hecker (1819–1888) formed the most influential delegation at the conference. Léonce-Fabre des Essarts (1848–1917), Gnostic bishop of Bordeaux, in a letter addressed to the archbishop of Paris under the name Synesius, wrote, "What we are preparing is neither a political assembly nor a council of heresiarchs, but the true ecumenical council of the new times."[227]

The pan-ecumenical projects failed and the Theosophical Society divided into two competing organizations: the Theosophical Society of Adyar, in India, which hosted the headquarters of the organization, and the Theosophical Society of America, with its seat in Altadena, California. From the former were derived the *Ordo Templi Orientis* and the Memphis-Misraim Rite of Theodor Reuss (1855–1923), of which

[227] Cit. in Msgr. Henri Delassus, *L'Américanisme ou la conjuration antichrétienne* [*Americanism or the Anti-Christian Conspiracy*], Éditions Saint-Rémi, Cadillac 2012 (1899), pp. 107–8.

the satanist Aleister Crowley (1875–1947) was a member. From the latter was born the Anthroposophical Society of Rudolf Steiner (1861–1925), which he presented as the "Theosophy of the West" because he did not place oriental doctrines in the foreground, as Blavatsky had done. However, for Anthroposophy, as for Theosophy and Hinduism, God is immanent to the world. Common to all the Theosophic sects is the sentiment of universal fraternity, beyond every religious faith, and the belief in reincarnation, or karma, which would allow the soul, after death, to liberate the god within us, so as to be reabsorbed in the universal One.[228]

4. The Diffusion of Antisemitism in Theosophical Settings

In her most renown book, *The Secret Doctrine* (1888), Hélène Blavatsky proposed a connection between "physical race" and spiritual attributes. Thus, in Theosophical settings, the Aryan myth arose, which saw in northern populations the bearers of creativity and vital strength, and in the Jews an inferior, degenerate race. The historian David S. Katz underlines, "Theosophy enjoyed great influence in Germany and Austria, where it integrated well with *Lebensreform,* the late-Romantic movement that emphasized various alternative lifestyles, including vegetarianism, herbal medicine, rural communes, and nudism."[229] This ideology, called *völkisch,* cultivated a pantheistic vision of the cosmos that harkened to the worship and myths of the ancient Germans, including worship of the sun and of natural forces.

[228] For a broad critique of this doctrine, see Francesco M. Gaetani, S.J., *L'uomo* [*Man*], Libreria della Pontificia Università Gregoriana, Rome 1946, pp. 238–352, and Paolo Siwek, S.J., *Eresie e superstizioni d'oggi* [*Heresies and Superstitions of Today*], Herder, Rome 1963, pp. 215–322.

[229] David S. Katz, *The Occult Tradition: From the Renaissance to the Present Day*, Pimlico, London 2007.

The Austrian novelist Guido von List (1848–1919) was the first to combine the *völkisch* ideology with occult and Theosophical concepts, promoting "Wotanism," a presumed Teutonic religion based on the esoteric knowledge of runes, the archaic writing of the ancient Norsemen. List drew inspiration from Madame Blavatsky, claiming he possessed a "secret science" that allowed him to rediscover the secret language of the ancient Germans, whose successor he considered himself. During the summer solstice of 1911, List founded the *Hoher Armanen-Orden* (HAO), the Supreme Order of the Armans, a secret society and custodian of the "sacred Gnosis" of the primitive Germans, transmitted by magicians in the Renaissance and by Rosicrucian and Masonic societies in their battle against the Catholic Church.

An ex-Cistercian monk named Jörg Lanz von Liebenfels (1874–1954), expelled from his order for moral reasons, took up List's cause. He fused the pagan sun worship with Theosophical conceptions and arrived at the belief that the Germanic peoples, nearer to a presumed physical and spiritual perfection of an Aryan type, would be the descendants of the mythical divine race of the Hyperboreans. Lanz von Liebenfels defined his Gnostic cosmogony "Theozoology," and the secret doctrine of the Aryans he termed "Ariosophy."

Rudolf Glauer (1875–1945), known as Rudolf von Sebottendorff, founded the Thule Secret Society in Munich in 1918, after having lived in Turkey where he had affiliated himself with a Masonic lodge. Many future members of the National Socialist Party were to belong the Thule Society. In 1933, he wrote a book titled *Before Hitler Came,* in which he documented the relations of the Thule Society with the Nazi Party.[230] Theodor Fritsch (1852–1933)

[230] Rudolf von Sebottendorff, *Prima che Hitler venisse. Storia della Società Thule* [*Before Hitler Came: History of the Thule Society*], tr. It. Edizioni Delta-Arktos, Turin 1987, with an introduction by Renato Del Ponte.

belonged to the Thule as well. In 1912 he founded in Munich the *Germanenorden,* a para-Masonic Grand Lodge whose members dressed in white and wore horned helmets. Among the symbols they used appears the swastika, one of the Thule symbols later adopted by the National Socialists.

The influence of these Theosophical groups on National Socialism has been studied by numerous historians of various nationalities and cultural backgrounds. Among the more reliable of these, we point out George Mosse (1918–1999), who dedicated an ample study to *The Cultural Origins of the Third Reich;*[231] Nicholas Goodrick-Clarke (1953–2012), author of an equally important volume dedicated to *The Occult Roots of Nazism;*[232] and the Italian political scientist Giorgio Galli (1928–2020), who researched the magic-esoteric component of Hitlerian doctrine in numerous books.[233]

According to Nicholas Goodrick-Clarke, "the strident anti-Catholicism of Ariosophy" can be traced back to the pan-Germanic influence of Georg von Schönerer (1842–1921), who already in 1898 had launched his campaign *Los von Rom* (*Break with Rome*).[234] Goodrick-Clarke highlights the bonds of Theozoological Gnosis and Ariosophy with the monism of Ernst Heinrich Haeckel (1834–1919), which, "on the solid base of comparative zoology," proposed a religion of nature as an alternative to the "irrational" dualistic religions of the past.[235] The historian Daniel E. Gasman (1933–2012)

231 George Mosse, *The Crisis of German Ideology: Intellectual Origins of the Third Reich*, University of Wisconsin Press, Madison 2021.

232 Nicholas Goodrick-Clarke, *The Occult Roots of Nazism: Secret Aryan Cults and Their Influence on Nazi Ideology*, Tauris Parke, London 2019.

233 Giorgio Galli, *Hitler e il nazismo magico* [*Hitler and Magical Nazism*], Rizzoli, Milan 2019; *Hitler e la cultura occulta* [*Hitler and Occult Culture*], Rizzoli, Milan 2013.

234 N. Goodrick-Clarke, *The Occult Roots of Nazism*, pp. 27–28.

235 Ibid., pp. 151–52.

established an irrefutable parallel between the social Darwinism of Haeckel and National Socialist ideology.[236]

On January 30, 1933, Hitler received from President Hindenburg the office of Reich Chancellor. As his appointment for the "surveillance" of ideological education of the party and of all the associations aligned with it, he nominated Alfred Rosenberg (1893–1945), the man who represented "the quintessence of all the powers present in the National Socialist Party hostile to the Church and to Christianity."[237] Rosenberg was placed in charge of the newspaper *Beobachter* which the Nazi Party had acquired in 1920 from the Thule Society at the behest of Dietrich Eckart (1868–1923), a member of the secret society who exercised a strong influence over Hitler.

The antisemitic and antichristian persecution by National Socialism was the logical consequence of a vision of the world founded on Theosophic and neopagan doctrines that inspired the movement.

5. The Church and the Condemnation of Antisemitism

The manifesto of National Socialism, *The Myth of the Twentieth Century*[238] by Alfred Rosenberg, was placed on the Index by the Church on February 7, 1934. On March 14, 1937, Pius XI issued his encyclical *Mit brennender Sorge*, in which the pope openly condemned "the myth

[236] Daniel Gasman, *The Scientific Origins of National Socialism: Social Darwinism in Ernst Haeckel and the German Monist League*, MacDonald, London 1971; Ibid., *Haeckel's Monism and the Birth of Fascist Ideology*, Lang, New York 1998.

[237] Hans-Ulrich Thamer, *Il terzo Reich. La Germania dal 1933 al 1945* [*The Third Reich: Germany from 1933 to 1945*], tr. It. Il Mulino, Bologna 1993, p. 550.

[238] Alfred Rosenberg, *Der Mythus des 20. Jahrhunderts. Eine Wertung der seelisch-geistigen Gestaltenkämpfe unserer Zeit* [*The Myth of the Twentieth Century: An Evaluation of the Mental-Spiritual Gestalt Struggles of Our Time*], Hoheneichen Verlag, Munich 1930.

of blood and race," affirming moreover, "if race or people, if the state or a determinate form of it, if the representatives of state power or other fundamental elements of human society have in the natural order a place both essential and worthy of respect; whoever moreover detaches them from this ladder of earthly values, elevating them to the supreme norm of all things, even over religious values, and divinizing them with idolatrous worship , perverts and falsifies the order created and imposed by God, is far from the true faith in God and from a conception of life in conformity to it."[239] "Only superficial spirits can fall into the error of speaking of a national God, of a national religion, and undertake the deranged attempt to imprison within the limits of but one people, in the ethnic narrowness of but one race, God, Creator of the world, king and legislator of peoples, before whose greatness the nations are as little as drops in a basin of water."[240]

In those years, Plinio Corrêa de Oliveira did not fail to denounce Nazi antisemitism in the pages of the journal *O Legionario*, demonstrating the substantial difference with the measures of prudence and precaution taken historically by the Church with regard to the Jewish people. "But this precaution is directed exclusively toward the doctrinal errors of the Jews and not against their race as such, which is the race into which the Word was incarnated. When sincerely converted, the Jew is a beloved son of the Church,"[241] which has always declared "with incessant energy, that the ancient people of God should never be without our charity. Nazism, to the contrary, offered the Jews only brutal and senseless cruelty."[242]

239 Pio XI, Enc. *Mit brennender Sorge* of March 14, 1937, in *Enchiridion delle Encicliche. Pio XI* (1922–1939), EDB, Bologna 1995, p. 1083.

240 Ibid., p. 1085.

241 Plinio Corrêa de Oliveira, "Uma velha ambição dos Judeus" [An Old Jewish Ambition], in *O Legionário*, no. 308 (August 7, 1938).

242 Ibid., "7 dias em rivista" [Seven Days in Review], in *O Legionário*, no. 232 (February 21, 1937).

Msgr. Antonino Romeo's thorough entry "Antisemitism" in the *Catholic Encyclopedia*[243] documents how the theological position of the Church with regard to the Jews has nothing to do with antisemitism. The charity of the Church toward the Jewish people, explains the theologian Pier Carlo Landucci (1900–1986), is nothing less than the truth of the Gospel, founded on the absolute certainty of the Christian faith in the divinity of Christ. The Jewish people, "preferred, not due to their current state, but to their initial election," remains "the prodigal son long-awaited by divine mercy."[244]

We recall the apostolate of the brothers Augustin and Joseph Lémann, twins who were Ashkenazi Jews (1836–1909/1915), orphans raised by uncles and aunts in a wealthy Jewish family of Lyon. On their spontaneous initiative, they were baptized and entered the Catholic Church. The twins then became priests, theologians, and honorary canons of various basilicas and cathedrals, monsignors by will of St. Pius X, and authors (both coauthoring and individually) of about one hundred and fifty publications; in 1892 they founded in Haifa the convent of Our Lady of Mount Carmel.

The Lémann brothers played a key role at the First Vatican Council, where they circulated a *Postulatum pro Hebreis* that was signed by almost all the Council Fathers, with the support of Pius IX. The aim of the *Postulatum* was to obtain from the council a heartfelt and merciful appeal to the Jewish people, calling them to conversion.[245] Only the outbreak of the Franco-Prussian War,

[243] Msgr. Antonino Romeo, *Antisemitismo* [*Antisemitism*], in *Enciclopedia Cattolica*, vol. I (1948), col. 1494–1505.

[244] Msgr. Pier Carlo Landucci, *Miti e realtà* [*Myth and Reality*], La Roccia, Rome 1968, p. 442; "La véritable charité envers le peuple juif" [True Charity for the Jewish People], in *La Pensée Catholique*, no. 207 (1983), pp. 13–31.

[245] Joseph and Augustin Lémann, *La cause des restes d'Israel, introduite au concile oecuménique du Vatican sous la bénédiction de S.S. le pape Pie IX* [*The Cause of the Remnant of Israel, introduced at the Vatican Ecumenical*

which concluded Vatican I prematurely, impeded the official promulgation of the *Postulatum*.

Antisemitism is the fruit of a deformed philosophy of history. To the Augustinian concept of the Two Cities and to the Ignatian concept of the Two Flags, that of Jesus Christ, "High Captain of the Good," and that of Lucifer, "head of the adversaries" of Christ,[246] National Socialism substitutes a cosmic war between blood and gold, between race and plutocracy, a word that entered into the political lingo of the twentieth century to indicate the predominance of financial oligarchs in the life of society. This perspective is extraneous to Christianity because it sees not ideas, but economic interests, as the guiding forces of history.

6. The Protocols of the Learned Elders of Zion

The anti-plutocratic doctrines found an instrument of propaganda in a presumed Jewish plan to control the world known as the *Protocols of the Learned Elders of Zion*. The *Protocols* were published for the first time in Russia in 1903 in the newspaper *Znamia* (The Flag) and, after two anonymous editions, in 1905 it was published in St. Petersburg in a volume edited by Sergej Aleksandrovič Nilus (1862–1929), as the last chapter in his book on the advent of the Antichrist. The diffusion of this text was vast, and the literature dedicated to it was equally wide. The *Protocols* are, by unanimous agreement, a forgery, compiled using at times verbatim texts as diverse as the *Dialogues in Hell Between Machiavelli and Montesquieu* (1864) by the Parisian attorney Maurice Joly (1829–1879), the novel *Biarritz* (1868) by the German journalist Hermann Goedsche (1815–1878),

Council under the blessing of H.H. Pope Pius IX], Socii Sancti Michaelis, Ghent 1980 (1912).

[246] S. Ignazio, *Esercizi Spirituali, Meditazione delle due bandiere* [*Spiritual Exercises, Meditation of the Two Flags*], n. 138.

but also the libelous work of Osman Bey (1836–1901) *The World Conquest of the Jews*. The most thorough investigation of this falsification was carried out by the Slavic scholar Cesare De Michelis (1943–2018), in a study titled *The Inexistent Manuscript,* which differs from other works on the subject in that it does not focus on the diffusion of the text, but on its historical and linguistic reconstruction.[247]

De Michelis debunks the version still widespread, according to which the forgery was compiled by Pyotr Rachkovsky (1853–1910), head of the French section of the Okhrana, the Tsar's secret police. He attributes, on the other hand, the paternity of the document to a group of pan-Slavists of the "Russian Circle," including Georgij Vasil'evic Butmi de Kacman (1858–1918), Mikhail Osipovich Menshikov (1859–1918), and Pavel Alexandrovic Krusevan (1869–1909). The thesis of De Michelis was confirmed by the discovery of the original print of the *Protocols* by the Russian historian Ljubov' Vladimirovna Ul'janova-Bibliko from the State University of Moscow, from which emerges the undeniable responsibility of Georgij Butmi for the redaction of the text.[248]

The *Protocols* were spread throughout the rest of Europe by expatriate Russians after the October Revolution. In Germany, after a first edition in 1919, Alfred Rosenberg edited a second in 1923. Adolf Hitler cited the *Protocols* in *Mein Kampf* and, based on this document as well, developed the thesis of the international Jewish plot against the Aryan race. In Italy, the *Protocols* were publicized by Giovanni Preziosi (1881–1945). The magazine he directed, *La Vita*

[247] Cf. Cesare De Michelis, *Il manoscritto inesistente. I «Protocolli dei savi di Sion»* [*The Non-Existent Manuscript: The Protocols of the Learned Elders of Zion*], Marsilio, Venice 2004.

[248] Id., "Protocolli dei savi di Sion. Ritrovato il protografo" [Protocols of the Learned Elders of Zion: The Original Rediscovered], in *Studi Slavistici*, XVIII (2022), pp. 253–55.

Italiana (Italian Life), published them in 1938, in the fifth edition, with an introduction by Julius Evola (1898–1974), who expressed himself thus: "If (and only if) the *Protocols* were not 'authentic' in the narrowest sense of the word, it is as if they were so for two capital and decisive reasons: because the facts demonstrate the truth; because their correspondence with the mother-ideas of traditional and modern Judaism is uncontestable."[249]

Intellectual criticism of the "mother-ideas of international Judaism" is naturally licit, but what is arbitrary is the pretense of basing this criticism on a document of which one admits the possible falsification. The renunciation of considering the authenticity of the document indicates an abandonment of the objective criteria of true and false, which must apply to the philosopher, as to the historian or the philologist. Evola thus enters the tunnel of relativism, in which truth does not matter, but only what is functional to the thesis one wants to demonstrate and, insofar as it works, it *becomes* "true." True, or "plausible," in the pretense of telling something that is similar to reality, often and easily deforms that reality.

In the case of the *Protocols,* if the historical and philological analysis of the text demonstrates its falsity, Christian philosophy of history demonstrates the implausibility of it as well. The documents of authentic conspirators, such as Weishaupt or Buonarroti, do not reveal a simple thirst for power or financial avidity, but express a metaphysical vision of reality that is absent from the *Protocols of the Learned Elders of Zion.*

The *Protocols* appear to be a forgery from their ambivalent nature: on one side, they were used to justify the National Socialist persecution against the Jews, on the basis of their presumed veracity;

[249] Julius Evola, *Introduzione ai Protocolli dei Savi Anziani di Sion* [*Introduction to the Protocols of the Learned Elders of Zion*], La Vita Italiana, Rome 1938, pp. 9–10.

on the other, on the basis of their falsity, they were used to affirm the inexistence of any plot of conspiracy whatsoever in history. It is true that the *Protocols* foresaw some things that came about, beginning with the project of the construction of a universal republic. Nevertheless, these predictions were widespread in the history of political and social ideas at that time. Victor Hugo, for example, spoke with a prophetic tone of the "universal republic" in a more explicit manner than even the *Protocols,* as in his renowned discourse on August 21, 1849, dedicated to the "United States of Europe."[250]

The globalist project belongs to a variety of social utopians who designed it beginning in the age of Renaissance humanist, from More to Campanella, from Condorcet and Saint-Simon, all the way to the League of Nations, to the "global village" and the Internet, as Armand Mattelart has well demonstrated in his *History of Planetarian Utopianism.*[251] The social fantasies of these utopians can be confuted without needing to find a conspiracy as equally imaginative.

7. *The Prague Cemetery* of Umberto Eco

Umberto Eco (1932–2016) was a professor of semiology who became famous in 1980 with his novel *The Name of the Rose.* At the center of this novel, as for the other five which followed it, is the theme of conspiracy, which Eco pretends to mystify in the name of an illumined rationalism. The plotting that Eco claims he wants to ridicule is, however, the main ingredient to the success of his books, all based on mysterious and absurd storylines.

The Prague Cemetery, published in 2010, deserves particular attention, because in this work Eco demonstrates a vast knowledge of

250 Victor Hugo, in "Le Siècle," August 23, 1849, in *Actes et paroles,* vol. I, *Avant l'exil: 1841–1851,* Michel Lévy Frères, Paris 1875, p. 383.

251 Armand Mattelart, *Storia dell'utopia planetaria. Dalla città profetica alla società globale* [*History of the Planetary Utopia: From the Prophetic City to the Global Society*], tr. It. Einaudi, Turin 2003.

the Catholic anti-Masonic literature and seems so obsessed by the possibility that it might express some truth that he seeks to demolish it by deconstructing the *Protocols of the Learned Elders of Zion,* with which this literature has no legitimate connection.

The Prague Cemetery speaks of the life of Simone Simonini, nephew of Giovan Battista Simonini, author of a letter that delineated the Jewish plans concerning world domination. This letter, sent to the *Abbé* Barruel, is real. The French Jesuit made private use of it only, and the text was published only after his death. In Eco's fiction, basing his narrative on the letter, after the death of the grandfather, the young Simonini begins elaborating a plot theory that uses the Jews as its scapegoat. Simonini specializes in the construction of false documents, and he disseminates them to the Jesuits, as well as German, Russian, and French secret service agents. Simonini the Younger, whom Eco marks in a final note as the only character in the book that he invented, encounters over the course of the novel's five-hundred pages innumerable actors from nineteenth century history: protagonists from the Italian Risorgimento Nino Bixio (1821–1873) and Ippolito Nievo (1831–1861), the nationalist journalist Edouard Drumont (1844–1917) and Colonel Ferdinand Walsin-Estherazy (1847–1923), the true guilty party in the Dreyfuss Affair; the ex-Freemason Léo Taxil (1854–1907) and the satanist priest Joseph-Antoine Boullan (1824–1893), down to Maurice Joly and Hermann Goedsche, the authors of the two texts that inspired the *Protocols of the Learned Elders of Zion,* whose process of creation and social dissemination the novel pretends to reconstruct.

Eco does not limit his efforts to sustaining the falsity of the *Protocols,* but is convinced of the possibility of falsifying any historical document. Eco writes, "Simonini was keen on the idea that his forgeries were, so to say, authentic."[252] He, like his master the notary Rebaudengo, produces copies of documents that never existed, but which could or should have existed.[253] On the other hand, "one who must forge documents must always document his work."[254] The falsifier must draw on true documents to produce false ones, such that once they are produced, they cease to be false. And therefore, if every document can be falsified, no document can pretend to be absolutely true.

But if no document is, *in se*, true, all documents are, at least potentially, false and if none are for certain true, it cannot be said of any that they are for certain false. In fact, to say that a document is false, there must be at least one true document, which is not the case, not so much because true documents do not factually exist, as because, for Eco, truth itself does not exist, as such. With this we reach the heart of Eco's discourse: an absolute relativism that claims to dissolve not so much philosophical truth, as that of the facts which constitute the objective storyline of history.

Eco pushes his relativism to the point of considering true and false as correlative, not only on the philosophical and moral plane, but also on the factual plane. But if the historical forgery is indistinguishable from the true, only the good word of the forger and his accomplices will be able to attest to the non-veracity of the forgery. However, this is the good word of the same counterfeiter who, lying, can also attest to the veracity of the forgery or the non-veracity of the true. With this, Eco restores historical dignity to the *Protocols of the Learned Elders of Zion*, because if everything can be falsified and nothing exists that is true for certain, the truth is nothing but the subjective mask of a specific interest. True is that to which the document attributes truth.

252 Umberto Eco, *Il cimitero di Praga* [*The Prague Cemetery*], Bompiani, Milan 2010, p. 428.

253 Ibid., pp. 104–5.

254 Ibid., p. 121.

If, as Eco writes, "one need only speak of something to make it exist,"[255] one should ask if defining a document as false is sufficient to place its existence in doubt and, consequently, if his book will contribute to reducing the number of those who will read the *Protocols of the Learned Elders of Zion* or rather contribute to increasing them, stimulating their morbid curiosity. To destroy a document, in fact, it is not enough to demonstrate that it is false; one must show that it is improbable, given that, as Eco himself says, "people only believe in what they know"[256] and hold to be false only what they do not want to know, unless they are shown its improbability. The counterfeiter, in order to be believed, must produce a probable document. But what is probable can do without the document to be believed. In the final analysis, there remains the criterion of an interest, noble or ignoble as it may be. And for Eco, there exists nothing noble, because the human comedy is a succession of lies, extortions, homicides, hidden intrigues, and maneuvers of every sort.

The historian Anna Foà perceptively noted in the monthly *Pagine Ebraiche*: "If from the point of view of his novel, this procedure can be very captivating, from the point of view of history, the forgery seems to become true in a context in which all documents are forgeries, all are doubles or triples, and the confusion between false and true reigns sovereign.... When the construction of the forgery becomes the only truth, is it still possible to have any certainties, that for example which claims that the *Protocols of the Learned Elders of Zion* are a forgery created on purpose to strike the Jews, or does the perverse fascination of this antisemitic counterfeiter prevail in the end? Ultimately, does not Eco's construction, aimed at dismantling a forgery, end up, by some strange unintended consequence, reconstructing it?"[257]

255 Ibid., p. 385.

256 Ibid., p. 96.

257 Anna Foà, "La micidiale macchina del falso" [The Fatal Machine of the Forgery], in *Bokertov*, October 20, 2010.

8. The *Abbé* Augustin Barruel and Giovanni Battista Simonini

If re-establishing the truth is a task for the historian, we need to affirm vigorously that anyone who, like Umberto Eco, Norman Cohn, and many others, claims that the myth of the global Jewish conspiracy can be traced back to the *Abbé* Augustin Barruel is himself a counterfeiter.[258]

Barruel dedicates the first volume of his *Mémoires* to the *sophists de l'impiété,* the philosophers of the Enlightenment; the second volume to the *sophists de la rébellion,* namely the Freemasons of high degree; the third and fourth volumes to the *sophists de l'anarchie,* who include the Bavarian Illuminati and the occult disciples of Emanuel Swedenborg and Louis-Claude de Saint-Martin. Missing in all his volumes is any reference to the Jews. When, after the publication of his work, Barruel received a letter from Giovanni Battista Simonini that affirmed having received some confidences about the harmful role of the Jews in the society of his age, he behaved with extreme prudence, so much so that this letter was known of only in 1882, when antisemitism had already spread throughout Europe.

Joseph-Arthur de Gobineau (1816–1882) published in 1853–1854 his *Essai sur l'inégalité des races humaines,* from which the exalter of the Germanic race Houston Stewart Chamberlain (1855–1927) drew; Ernest Renan (1823–1922), in 1855, published a *Histoire générale et système des languages sémitiques,* in which he contrasted the Aryan race, heir of pagan polytheism, with semitic Judeo-Christianity; the materialist and positivist philosopher Eugen Du (1833–1921), published in 1881, a year before the letter of Simonini came to light, the tract *The Jewish Question as a Racial,*

[258] Norman Cohn, *Warrant for Genocide: The Myth of the Jewish World-Conspiracy and the Protocols of the Elders of Zion,* Harper and Row, New York 1967.

Moral, and Cultural Problem. All of these works were extraneous to the cultural horizon of the Jesuits and of the Catholic Church.

Furthermore, from 1880 onward, a *Deutsche Reformpartei* (DRP) existed in Germany, characterized by strong antisemitism. Theodor Fritsch, later founder of the *Germanenorden* and the first German translator of the *Protocol of the Learned Elders of Zion*, was a member of this party. The context that gave birth to modern antisemitism was pagan and antichristian, and has nothing to do with the Catholic counter-revolutionary tradition.

But who was Giovanni Battista Simonini, in reality? An unsigned article in the *Civiltà Cattolica*, from October 12, 1882, contained "a curious document, never published to date, as far as we know." The *Abbé* Barruel recalls having received, on August 20, 1806, a letter written in Florence on August 10 by a soldier of the Savoys, a certain Giovanni Battista Simonini, who after having complimented him for the richness and precision of his work, provided him some information, based on confidences received in Masonic circles, on the Jewish influence in the world. Simonini had entered a lodge in Turin and had learned that the Jews were the founders of Freemasonry and other sects and that they had a growing influence on contemporary life. Among the various news items reported in Simonini's letter, there is one according to which "in Italy alone, they (the Jews) enjoyed the support of more than eight hundred ecclesiastics, both diocesan and religious, among whom were many parish priests, public professors, prelates, some bishops, and a few cardinals; and that for some time they no longer despaired of having a pope in their party."[259]

Barruel communicated a copy of the letter to the ministers of the Napoleonic police and sent the original to Pope Pius VII himself, "praying him to find sufficient and convenient information on

[259] Contemporary news stories, in *Civiltà Cattolica*, series XI, vol. XII (1882), p. 222 (pp. 219–28).

Simonini to judge the degree of trust the letter merited." Several months later, the pope, informed in Florence about Simonini, sent word to Barruel "that everything led us to believe in the veracity and probity" of the soldier of the Savoys. Barruel entrusted another letter to a brother of a confraternity Fidèle de Grivel (1769–1842), who, a few years later, took it with him to Maryland, where it was tracked down at the end of the nineteenth century by another confraternity brother Ivan Gagarin (1814–1882), who published it with the other *souvenirs* Fr. Grivel had on Barruel.[260]

Giovanni Battista Simonini really did exist and, as Paolo Bianchini has demonstrated, played an important role in an episode that took place in Turin on May 26, 1799.[261] Simonini, born in 1744 or 1745, had taken part in a volunteer urban militia that opposed the French invasion of Piedmont from 1793 until their capitulation on December 8, 1798. When, in 1799, the Russian and Austrian troops under General Suvorov besieged the city, Simonini, with a group of friends, took advantage of the confusion and opened the city gate to the anti-French army, which was able to enter the Savoy capital with minimal resistance. Later he entered the *Amicizia Cristiana* (Christian Friendship), the secret counter-revolutionary society founded by Fr. Nikolaus von Diessbach (1732–1798) and directed in Turin by the venerable Pio Brunone Lanteri (1759–1830). *Amicizia Cristiana*, constituted by Fr. Luigi Virginio (1756–1805), together with Fr. Barruel, was probably

[260] Ivan Gagarin, *Souvenirs du P. Grivel sur les PP: Barruel et Feller* [*Fr. Grivel's Memories of Fr. Barruel and Fr. Feller*] in "Le Contemporain", t. XXX (1878), pp. 49–70.

[261] Paolo Bianchini, "L'uso politico del mito: il complotto giudaico in Europa tra Settecento e Ottocento" [The Political Use of Myth: The Jewish Plot in Europe in the 1700s and 1800s] in *Alfabetizzazione, scolarizzazione e processi formativi nell'arco alpino. Itinerari di studio, temi di ricerca e prospettive d'intervento* [*Literacy, Schooling, and Educational Processes in the Alps: Study Itineraries, Research Themes and Perspectives for Intervention*], ed. by Paolo Sibilla and Giorgio Chiosso, Libreria Stampatori, Turin 2005, pp. 149–72.

the channel through which Simonini had his letter passed on to the French Jesuit, which was read during a meeting of *Amicizia Cattolica* in Turin on October 15, 1821, according to the minutes of that association.[262] The public divulgation of the letter of the *Abbé* Barruel did not take place before 1882, however.

All of this is simply history.

9. The Myth of the "New World"

There is a spirit of evil that seems to permeate the revolutionary ideologies and the totalitarianisms of the twentieth century. These draw their origin from a common faith in a "new world," which would be possible to inaugurate on this earth and which would liberate humanity from the evils that afflict it. This idea was expressed by the "New World Order" proposed by Woodrow Wilson (1856–1924), a liberal Democrat, in the journal *L'Ordine nuovo* (The New Order), organ of the Italian Communist Party of Antonio Gramsci (1891–1937), and of the geo-political theory of a "New Order" (*Neuordnung*), which Adolf Hitler wanted to impose on Europe.

The political philosopher Eric Voegelin (1901–1985) defined as "new Gnosis" the modern myth of the "new world," which entrusts to man the utopia of a "global redemption" of humanity.[263] The Gnostic conviction that the order of being, intrinsically evil, can be changed and substituted in history by a "new world" was tragically shattered in its crash into reality.

[262] Candido Bona, *Le Amicizie, società segrete e rinascita religiosa (1770–1830) [The Friendships, Secret Societies, and Religious Rebirth (1770–1830)],* Deputazione Subalpina di Storia Patria, Turin 1962, p. 581. See also R. de Mattei, *La biblioteca delle "Amicizie": repertorio critico della cultura cattolica nell'epoca della Rivoluzione, 1770–1830* [*The Library of the "Friendships": Critical Repertory of Catholic Culture in the Epoch of the Revolution, 1770–1830*], Bibliopolis, Naples 2005.

[263] Eric Voegelin, *Il mito del mondo nuovo* [*The Myth of the New World*], Rusconi, Milan 1970.

The twentieth century, the epoch in which the New World Order was to come about, was the most destructive century in all of human history, the century in which for the first time terms such as "genocide" or "democide" appear,[264] the latter being a term coined by Rudolph Joseph Rummel (1932–2014) to indicate the intentional killing on the part of the government of unarmed people or populations, committed by international governments not directly ascribable to the category of genocide.[265]

It is not our intention here to write a history of *congiure* and conspiracies of the twentieth century. There were *congiure* that failed, like that of July 20, 1944, organized by a narrow group of German officers against Hitler, and *congiure* that succeeded, like that of July 25, 1943, against Mussolini. There were other *congiure,* or conspiracies, still shrouded in mystery, like the assassination of John F. Kennedy on November 22, 1963, and the assassination attempt on John Paul II on May 13, 1981.

The self-dissolution of the Soviet Union from 1989 to 1991 raises even more questions. The demise of National Socialism in 1945 was sealed by the suicide of Hitler in his Berlin bunker and by the Nuremburg Trials of those responsible for National Socialism. The fall of Communism, on the other hand, occurred painlessly, without insurrections and rebellions, almost acquiesced to by those who ought to have resisted the fall.

Anatoliy Golitsyn[266] (1926–2008), an ex-officer in the KGB who defected to the West, claimed that *perestroika* and the consequent

[264] See Marco Revelli, *Oltre il Novecento* [*Beyond the 1900s*], Einaudi, Turin 2001, pp. 7–12; M. Flores et al., *Il genocidio. Declinazioni e risposte di inizio secolo* [*Genocide: Variations and Responses from the Beginning of the Century*], Giappichelli, Turin 2018.

[265] Rudolph J. Rummel, *Death by Government*, Transaction Publisher, New Brunswick 1994, tr. It. *Stati assassini. La violenza omicida dei governi*, Rubbettino, Soveria Mannelli 2005, pp. 47–49.

[266] Anatoliy Golitsyn, *New Lies for Old*, Dodd, Mead and Co., New York 1984; Golitsyn, *The Perestroika Deception*, Edward Harle, London 1995.

self-dissolution of the USSR was the result of a carefully studied design, something confirmed by Vladimir Bukovsky (1942–2019), author of a historical work, *The Secret Archives of Moscow*, in which, on the basis of thousands of documents of the Central Committee of the Communist Party in the USSR, he attributes to Kremlin leaders the liquefaction of the Soviet empire, when they realized their system was on the verge of a grave structural crisis.[267] The revelation of this strategic plan had no echo in the media while, around the Islamic attack on the Twin Towers on September 11, 2001, there developed the political fiction theory of an American–Zionist *congiura*, which constituted one of the sources of the conspiracy theories in the coronavirus epoch.

10. The New Age and the Conspiracy of Aquarius

The fall of the Berlin Wall in November of 1989, and the self-dissolution of the Soviet Union in the following two years, did not represent the mere end of a political system, but the twilight with it of the myth of progress, understood as the necessary linear evolution of humanity toward a better future. The "sense of history," the "scientific" nature of which Marxist-Leninism had assured its adherents, was suddenly foiled. From the wreckage of "real socialism" emerged a "weak" or "postmodern" school of thought which, without denying the final aims of Marxism, put in doubt its allegedly scientific premises. Hegel and Marx's philosophies of history were substituted by the "epistemological breakthrough" of the theorizers of "chaos,"[268] like the chemist Ilya Prigogine (1917–2003) and the sociologist Edgar Morin. According to the historian François Furet (1927–1997), "History becomes a tunnel where man enters in the dark, without knowing where his

[267] Vladimir Bukovsky, *Gli Archivi segreti di Mosca* [*The Secret Archives of Moscow*], Spirali, Milan 1999.

[268] R. de Mattei, *1900–2000. Due sogni si succedono. La costruzione, la distruzione* [*One Dream Follows Another: Construction, Destruction*], Edizioni Fiducia, Rome 1990.

actions will take him, uncertain of his own destiny, lacking the illusory security of a science of what he does. Without God, the democratic individual at the end of this century sees trembling from the foundations the 'divinity of history': an anxiety he must exorcise."[269]

This is the age which Plinio Corrêa de Oliveira defined as the "Fourth Revolution," characterized by the collapse of reason, "by now hypertrophied through the practice of placing all in doubt, by Cartesian thought, the divinization of the French Revolution, employed to the point of open abuse in every Communist school of thought."[270] It is in the context of this "extinction of old models of reflection, of volition and of individual sensibility, of thought and of deliberation that are increasingly collective," that they affirm the doctrines of the New Age.[271]

The American occultist Alice Bailey (1880–1949) claims that following the Allied victory in the Second World War, "the progress of humanity" would have brought about the "Age of Aquarius," in which traditional religions would be eliminated and substituted by a global, syncretistic religion.[272] These old Theosophic theses were inherited by the generation of the hippies who professed pacifism, universal harmony, and a pseudo-mystical religiosity to be attained even by means of hallucinogenic drugs.

The American journalist Marilyn Ferguson (1938–2008) theorized the advent of a New Age that would transform individuals and planetary society: "A powerful network, though without a leader, without a head, is working to provoke a radical change in the United

[269] François Furet, *Il passato di un'illusione. L'idea comunista nel XX secolo* [*The Past of an Illusion: The Communist Idea in the Twentieth Century*], Mondadori, Milan 1995, p. 559.

[270] P. Corrêa de Oliveira, *Rivoluzione e Contro-Rivoluzione* [*Revolution and Couter-Revolution*], p. 191.

[271] Ibid.

[272] Alice Bailey, *Discipleship in the New Age*, Lucis Publishing Company, New York 1944 and 1955.

States. Its members have abandoned some of the strongholds of Western thought and perhaps even the idea of historical continuity. This network is the Conspiracy of the Aquarius, an anomalous conspiracy without a political doctrine or a manifesto." It "has unleashed the fastest process of cultural reorganization in history."[273]

The sociologist Massimo Introvigne described the history of this movement from 1962 to 1992, which spread like a psychological ambient more than a proper doctrine.[274] The New Age "has tried to infiltrate practically every religious tradition, including Christianity, but found an environment in which it could live in a precise tradition, or perhaps in two: the Theosophic tradition and the magical-occultist tradition."[275] The historian of Gnosis Giovanni Filoramo traced the New Age back to the Gnostic paradigm that accompanies the history of esotericism, emphasizing that in its "consciousness of nature," "the self-realization of the individual is part of and facilitates, according to a typical modality of Gnosis, the self-realization of the Self or universal consciousness."[276]

Astrology, para-psychology, yoga, and Zen are all gathered up into a confused amalgam, in which each person takes or "imagines" that which most corresponds to their own curiosity. After 1968, the primacy of reason was substituted by that of "creative imagination," already theorized by the magicians of the Renaissance. But the field of the imagination is that in which demons can intervene altering the process of sensible knowledge. In fact, the demons who cannot act directly upon the intellective soul are able to act, as St. Thomas explains,

273 Marilyn Ferguson, *The Aquarian Conspiracy*, Paladin, London 1986, tr. It. *La cospirazione dell'Acquario*, Marco Tropea, Milan 1989, p. 21.

274 M. Introvigne, *Storia del New Age 1962–1992* [*History of the New Age 1962–1992*], Cristianità, Piacenza 1994.

275 Ibid., p. 29.

276 Giovanni Filoramo, "Tradizioni esoteriche e nuove forme di religione," in *L'Esoterismo* [*Esoteric Traditions and New Forms of Religion*], p. 708 (pp. 695–717).

on the senses and on the imaginative faculty, creating dreams at first individual which then become collective.[277]

Although it is not a "conspiracy" in the classical sense of the term, the New Age constitutes the psychological background of a subculture of the masses, of which the Internet has multiplied the damage, contributing to the creation of the plotting mentality of the late twentieth century. Introvigne rightly observes that beliefs such as that America never landed on the Moon, or that September 11 was provoked by international Zionism, are evidence of the new idea that popular culture (movies, novels, TV series) can be a source not only of entertainment, but also of hidden truths.[278]

The instruments which disseminate these theories are not limited to books, but include films or videos as well, like those of the journalist Giulietto Chiesa (1940–2020), *Zero: Investigation into September 11* (2007), and of the blogger Massimo Mazzucco, *11 September 2001: Global Deceit* (2006) and *September 11: The New Pearl Harbor* (2013). Chiesa was also known for disseminating theories about "chemtrails" and "artificial earthquakes," and Mazzucco for his support for theories of a "lunar conspiracy" (*Moon Hoax*), according to which the lunar landing never existed. Both evoked a "plot" against humanity when the Covid pandemic broke out at the start of 2020.

11. *The Da Vinci Code* and the "Reptilians"

If in the nineteenth and twentieth centuries the role of utopias was that of contrasting reality, anticipating an improbable future, dystopias were those that denounced the failure of classical utopias. Dystopia is an inverted utopia that does not usher in an imaginary Eden, but

277 Aquinas, *Quaestio disputata de malo*, q. 16, a. 11, resp.; q. 16, a. 9 ad primum.

278 M. Introvigne, *Nuove mitologie religiose* [*New Religious Mythologies*], in *XXI Secolo*, Istituto della Enciclopedia Italiana, Rome 2009, p. 659 (pp. 659–69).

the nightmares of the social inferno. The philosopher Massimo Baldini (1947–2008) dedicated a book to the *History of Utopias,* in which he wrote, "From dream to nightmare, from optimism to anthropological pessimism, from trust in progress to the death of hope in the future, from fancying a paradise of utopian perfection to their unmasking as horrible infernos. This was the place the utopian adventure in the twentieth century had reached."[279]

At the dawn of the twenty-first century, the passage from social utopias to dystopias received a great impulse from the diffusion of the works of the novelists Dan Brown and David Icke. *The Da Vinci Code* (2003), by the American Dan Brown, is a novel centered on the existence of a grand conspiracy that involves the Catholic Church. Robert Langdon, a scholar of symbolism, deciphers the destructive secret code which has attempted to transform humanity for centuries. The disturbing novelty is that Jesus Christ was a pagan for his entire life, without being God, and "was not only a husband, but also a father," and Mary Magdalene, his wife, was "the Holy Vase, namely, the chalice containing the real blood of Christ."[280] The Merovingian kings were the descendants of this marriage and their "royal blood" runs in the veins of the protagonist of the novel. Despite the absurdity and blasphemy of the thesis, the text has been perceived as a source of authentic information by millions of people and has fostered unimaginable enthusiasm for the apocryphal Gospels, especially the *Gospel of Judas,* a Gnostic text rediscovered in a cavern in Egypt in 1978. According to Brown, this text would include proof of the marriage of Jesus Christ and the Magdalene.

In the same years, millions of copies of books by the British writer David Icke, ex-soccer player and journalist, then spokesman

279 Massimo Baldini, *La storia delle utopie* [*The History of Utopias*], Armando, Rome 1994, p. 138.

280 Dan Brown, *The Da Vinci Code,* Doubleday, New York 2003, tr. It. *Il Codice da Vinci,* Mondadori, Milan 2016, p. 282.

for the English Green Party, were sold.[281] In these works, Icke claims that for millions of years a race of aliens from the remote planet Alpha Draconis have come to the earth to hold humanity captive.[282] These are the "reptilians," lizards that can transform from human appearance to that of enormous reptiles, through shapeshifting, or mutating their form. There are "pureblood" reptilians and "hybrid" ones, the fruit of a cross between reptilians and human beings. The pureblood reptilians, "who use the human body like an overcoat, in full awareness of their identity and of the plans they try to carry out,"[283] include members of the British royal family, several presidents of the United States, and other dynasties of magnates who dominate the economy, like the Rothschilds and the Rockefellers.

These characters, according to the "testimony" offered by Icke, are devoted to human sacrifice, drink human blood, and are protagonists of carnal violence on minors.[284] One of the global hubs of satanism is the "Castle of Darkness," near Muno Belm in Belgium, where rituals in honor of the satanic goddess Lilith are celebrated, alongside

[281] David Icke, *Figli di Matrix. Da migliaia di anni una razza proveniente da un'altra dimensione tiene soggiogata l'umanità… agendo sotto i nostri occhi* [*Children of the Matrix: For Thousands of Years a Race from Another Dimension Holds Humanity Captive… Agenda Right Under Our Eyes*], tr. It. Macro Edizioni, Diegaro di Cesena (Forlì) 2002.

[282] Icke, *Alice nel paese delle meraviglie e il disastro delle Torri Gemelle. Ecco perché la versione ufficiale dei fatti dell'11 settembre è una menzogna colossale* [*Alice in Wonderland and the Disaster of the Twin Towers: The Reason Why the Official Version of the Facts of September 11th Is an Enormous Lie*], tr. It. Macro Edizioni, Diegaro di Cesena (Forlì) 2003.

[283] Icke, *Il segreto più nascosto. Il libro che può cambiare la tua vita* [*The Best Hidden Secret: The Book That Can Change Your Life*], tr. it. Macro Edizioni, Diegaro di Cesena (Forlì) 2021, p. 49.

[284] Michael Barkun, *A Culture of Conspiracy: Apocalyptic Visions in Contemporary America*, University of California Press, Berkeley, Los Angeles, and London 2003.

demons of the Jewish Kabbalah, and "it seems that every day a child is sacrificed in the cellars."[285]

In Icke's cosmogony, "the Christian Church is a farce founded on a fiction . . . and that which is true of Christianity, counts for all the other religions as well: Judaism, Islam, Hinduism, and so forth."[286] Icke is convinced that 9/11 was a plot hatched by reptilians and that the Covid pandemic was organized to enslave humanity. It is no wonder he was among the promoters of the protests in London against lockdowns on September 26, 2020, and on July 21, 2021.

Aware of the absurdity of his theories, Icke suggests we do not "think with the intellect," but that we "feel" through the imagination the "revelation" that he proposes: "When we feel something we turn to the center of our heart, to our intuition, to the direct connection with the cosmos."[287] "Feeling" means learning to "think the unthinkable" or, we might say, to "believe the unbelievable." In order for our imagination to become real, it is enough to want it to.

12. QAnon and the Great Reset

Beginning in 2017, the virtual movement QAnon marked the irruption of conspiracy theories into political life. QAnon collected the followers of the revelations of an anonymous Internet user, denominated Q (anon is a shortened form of "anonymous user"), who passes himself off as an intelligence official appointed by the Pentagon to ensure that vital information, otherwise hidden, is handed on to the population. According to Q, there exists a hidden global government, the so-called Kabbalah, that took power in the United States after the assassination of John F. Kennedy and ever since controls the deep state, with the exception of the armed forces. The followers of QAnon

[285] D. Icke, *Il segreto più nascosto* [*The Best Hidden Secret*], p. 137.
[286] Ibid., p. 135.
[287] Ibid., p. 614.

claim, among other things, that the Kabbalah holds millions of children prisoners in an underground tunnel, after being kidnapped with the aim of sexually molesting them and drinking their blood to draw from it a psychotropic substance: the adrenochrome that would confer a sort of rejuvenation to those using it. QAnon seeks to "awaken" the people held in a mental stupor by the deep state and incapable of understanding the hidden plot that sustains the world.

Despite the extraordinary affirmations and predictions never realized, these theories saw incredible success during the Covid pandemic, considered by QAnon an instrument of the cabal to enslave humanity. On January 6, 2021, the QAnon movement had concrete visibility via the image of Jack Angeli, the "QAnon Shaman" who guided the invasion of the United States Capitol, and who was condemned to forty-one months in jail. Shamanism is a para-religious technique characteristic of primitive cultures that permits an "initiate" to enter into contact with the world of spirits by means of an altered state of consciousness.[288] The myth of the shaman, as an interlocutor of an extra-human world, was launched by the New Age and is today present among the adherents of QAnon and of other occult sects.

One of the most fervent Italian followers of QAnon explains that "the dictatorship we are living in was founded on the principle of the Matrix, the virtual system described in the film of the same name. All those who are connected to this system believe that everything they are shown is effectively the truth and they do not realize, and in a certain sense they do not want to know, that the truth offered by power is nothing but an enormous lie. This system can function if everyone continues to believe blindly in the lie and does not step out of the Matrix, precisely. To step out of the Matrix there is only one way, and it is

[288] Cf. Mircea Eliade, *Lo sciamanesimo e le tecniche dell'estasi* [*Shamanism and the Techniques of Ecstasy*], tr. It. Mediterranee, Rome 1988 (1951).

that of taking the 'red pill.' The greater the number of people that take the red pill, the more people will leave the illusion and will begin to see the truth that the system has lied about for years."[289]

The Matrix is a science-fiction film directed in 1999 by the brothers Andy and Larry Wachowski, in which the human race is controlled and exploited by machines that make men believe they are living free, while in reality they keep humanity imprisoned to harvest from them the energy necessary for their survival. The red pill of knowledge awakens one to the world as it really is, while the blue pill condemns one to the imaginary world. Morpheus, one of the protagonists of the film, addresses another character he is trying to draw out of the dream he believes is reality: "This is your last chance, if you pass it up you won't have another. Blue pill, end of the story: tomorrow you'll wake up in your bedroom and you'll believe in whatever you want. Red pill, you stay in Wonderland, and you'll see how deep the hole of the white rabbit is. I'm just offering you the truth, remember that. Nothing more."

The white rabbit of *The Matrix* alludes to Lewis Carroll's (1832–1898) second novel *The Adventures of Alice in Wonderland* (1865), in which the protagonist falls through a rabbit hole into a fantastic world peopled by strange anthropomorphic creatures. The red pill is the metaphor of the "awakening," the "spark of consciousness" of ancient Gnostics reproposed by modern media.

Eric Davis, in *TechGnosis,* treated the topic of the so-called "Gnosis of the media," in a line that runs from the inventor of the concept of the noosphere, Teilhard de Chardin, to the theorist of collective intelligence, Pierre Lévy. The postmodern magicians

289 Cesare Sacchetti, "L'Italia al bivio: verso la fine della dittatura mondialista o verso il Grande Reset di Davos?" [Italy at a Crossroads: Towards the End of Global Dictatorship or Towards the Great Reset of Davos?], in *La Cruna dell'Ago.*

are the "wizards of chaos" who work on the Internet and live on their computers.[290]

The conspiracy fantasy takes hold in a society that is incapable of offering religious and moral certainties and so leaves room for what each feels and wants to believe. It is the age defined as "post-truth," in which the news is perceived and accepted as true by the public on the basis of emotions and sensations, without any concrete analysis of the effective reality of the facts narrated. In a discussion characterized by "post-truth," the objective facts (when clearly scrutinized) are less influential in forming public opinion than appeals to emotions and personal convictions. What prevails is the criteria not of reliability, but narrative effectiveness.[291]

It was as if this atmosphere of dogmatic credulity just materialized during the Covid pandemic. From the first months of 2020, a new "plot theory" began to emerge on social networks, according to which the pandemic must have been a global coup d'état, planned by the financial elite that controls national governments and public and private institutions to enslave all humanity. The coronavirus was just a mild influenza and the measures recommended by progressive and conservative governments of the whole world — lockdowns, masking, social distancing, and vaccines — were just instruments and symbols of this plot to confine citizens, tracing them with microchips, subjecting them to a health dictatorship, and finally exterminating all humanity. The financial elites and world leaders planned the non-existent pandemic to provoke a state of emergency that would allow a planetary restructuring of society: the so-called Great Reset. Robert F. Icke repeated this in London, Robert F. Kennedy Jr.

[290] Eric Davis, *TechGnosis. Miti, magia e misticismo nell'era dell'informazione* [*TechGnosis: Myths, Magic, and Mysticism in the Information Age*], Ipermedium Libri, Naples 2001, p. 197.

[291] Anna Maria Lorusso, *Postverità* [*Post-Truth*], Laterza, Bari-Rome 2018, p. 119.

in Berlin and Milan, while social media personalities competed with each other to amplify their voices.

As architects of this plot, one indicates generic financial elites exemplified by names such as Bill Gates, founder of Microsoft and of the Bill and Melinda Gates Foundation. But the only evidence leveled against Gates is that he is part of the establishment, with a circular argument that says the conspiracy is organized by a plutocratic elite, of which Gates is the representative, and the fact that Gates is part of this elite would constitute evidence of the existence of the conspiracy.

This reasoning in which the premises derive from the consequences, and these from those, thus creates a vicious circle where the demonstration is only apparent. The affirmation that must be demonstrated is a given in the reasoning that ought, on the contrary, to demonstrate that it is true.

The only evidence offered by theorists of a health conspiracy is *Event 201,* an exercise carried out in October 2019, at the Johns Hopkins Center for Health Security, to simulate a pandemic; and the meeting of the World Economic Forum of June 3, 2020, at which Klaus Schwab presented a proposal for reconstructing the economy after the Covid pandemic. Both events were public and not secret, and no proposal was made which was not already known. Nevertheless, the fact that *Event 201* foresaw the possibility of a pandemic is presented as proof that the promoters had organized it, and the fact that Schwab had proposed to take advantage of the pandemic to propose a Great Reset or New World Order would constitute proof that the pandemic was in fact the realization of this project.

In reality, the New World Order was declared in a different manner by the Soviet Union, by democratic America, by Nazi Germany, long before the coronavirus pandemic, and does not belong to the history of secret societies, but to that of the failed political projects of the last century. Those who openly or discretely act in history have not stopped elaborating their plans of social engineering. However, the project proposed by Klaus Schwab and Thierry Malleret in the book *COVID-19: The Great Reset* is not hidden, but open and declared, and must be fought without needing to insert it into a macro-conspiracy that makes a mockery of it.[292]

13. The Origins of the "No-Vax" Movement

One of the reasons for the success of the theory of a health conspiracy was the support it received from the "no-vax" or "anti-vax" movement which has its cultural roots in a vision of the world that on one side places psycho-physical well-being as the primary concern of man, and on the other side, attributes illness to an ignorance of man's spiritual powers.

Two French scholars, Françoise Salvadori and Laurent-Henri Vignaud, trace the origins of the anti-vaccination movement back to the Theosophic and Naturist horizons that characterized above all Germany and England at the turn of the nineteenth century.[293] Among the names they recall one finds the president of the English section of the Theosophical Society Anna Kingsford (1846–1888), the founder of Anthroposophy Rudolf Steiner (1861–1925), and exponents of the *völkisch* movement such as Richard Ungewitter (1869–1958).[294]

Anna Kingsford, occultist and "animalist" *antelitteram*, connected vaccination to vivisection and proposed killing, by means of the magical arts, the scientists who carried out experiments on animals, in particular the physiologist Claude Bernard (1813–1878),

[292] Klaus Schwab and Thierry Malleret, *COVID-19: The Great Reset*, Forum Publishing, Geneva 2020.

[293] Françoise Salvadori, Laurent-Henri Vignaud, *Antivax — Résistance aux vaccins du XVIIIe siècle à nos jours* [*Antivax — Vaccine Resistance from the Eighteenth Century to the Present Day*], Vendemiaire, Paris 2021.

[294] Rudolf Steiner and Ita Wegman, *Elementi fondamentali per un ampliamento dell'arte medica secondo le conoscenze della scienza dello spirito* [*Fundamental Elements for the Enlargement of the Medical Arts According to the Knowledge of the Science of the Spirit*], Editrice Antroposofica, Milan 1997 (1925).

his understudy Paul Bert (1833–1886) and the founder of microbiology Louis Pasteur (1822–1895), against whom she prepared "death spells" through certain rituals. After having boasted of the death of Bernard and Bert, in 1887, Anna Kingsford went to Paris to concentrate her forces on the "vaccinator" Pasteur. "I killed Paul Bert, I killed Claude Bernard, and I am going to kill Louis Pasteur and after him, the entire tribe of vivisectionists, if I live long enough to do so," she wrote in her diary.[295] However, after having spent five hours in the rain near the Pasteur Institute, she was stricken by a severe case of pneumonia which led to her own death.

In those very years, an "occult war" was waged with spells and curses between Josef-Antoine Boullan, an occultist priest who practiced obscene and sacrilegious rites, and the satanist Stanislaus de Guaita (1861–1897), Grand Master of Kabbalistic Order of the Rosy Cross. The death of Boullan on January 4, 1893, was considered by the occultists to be death by magical arts perpetrated by de Guaita, who died, in turn, of a drug overdose.

The anti-vaccinationist Rudolf Steiner, after having been secretary of the German section of the Theosophical Society and director of the Memphis-Misraim Rite in Germany, founded Anthroposophy, a dissident Theosophical society headquartered in Dornach, Switzerland. Assisted by the Dutch doctor Ita Wegman (1876–1943), Steiner founded "Anthroposophical Medicine," which opposed vaccination, convinced that vaccination hindered man's spiritual evolution as well as the cycle of reincarnation.

Richard Ungewitter was one of the apostles of the antivaccination movement, but also one of the first organizers of the nudist movement, which became a popular practice in Germany in the early

[295] Edward Maitland, *Anna Kingsford: Her Life, Letters, Diary and Work*, George Redway, London 1896, vol. II, p. 268. See also Christine Ferguson, *Anna Kingsford and the Intuitive Science of Occultism*, in "Aries-Journal for the Study of Western Esotericism," 2021, pp. 1–22.

twentieth century.[296] Other names can be added to his such as the naturopath Adolf Just (1859–1936), founder of the sanatorium in Jungborn; Willibald Huntschel (1858–1947), who proposed to renew the Aryan race through polygamy practiced in the agricultural colonies of the Artaman League he founded; and Edgar Dacqué (1878–1945), an evolutionist who turned Darwinism upside-down, claiming that monkeys descended from "primordial man."[297] All were supporters of *Nacktkultur*, the "culture of nudism" connected to sun worship, symbol of a return to nature mysticism.

Ungewitter, a Nazi from the beginning, was convinced that vaccination was "a plot of Jewish doctors aiming to poison the blood of the German race."[298] Julius Streicher (1885–1946), one of the leaders of the National Socialist Party and editor of *Der Stürmer*, was like Ungewitter a great propagator of nudism and the author of a violent campaign against serums and vaccines, considered a Jewish invention to corrupt German blood. Streicher was part of the *Germanorden* and of the Thule Association and, like Rosenberg and other Nazi party officials, was condemned to death in Nuremberg in 1945 for crimes against humanity.

14. The Ideologues of Anti-Globalism

In Italy, some intellectuals of the left have sought to give greater cultural dignity to the vaccinationist plot theories against humanity. Giorgio Agamben, known for his anarchist philosophical work *Homo*

[296] Karl Eric Toepfer, *Empire of Ecstasy: Nudity and Movement in German Body Culture 1910–1935*, University of California Press, Berkeley 1998, pp. 30–38; John Alexander Williams, *Turning to Nature in Germany: Hiking, Nudism, and Conservation, 1900–1940*, Stanford University Press, Redwood City 2007.

[297] Cf. Florian Mildenberger, "Drachen und Dämonen. Der Paläontologe Edgar Dacqué (1878–1945) Zwischen Wissenschaft und Mythologie" [Dragons and Demons: The Paleontologist Edgar Dacqué (1878–1945) Between Knowledge and Mythology], in *Zeitschrift für Geschichtswissenschaft*, 57 (2009), pp. 869–90.

[298] Salvadori and Vignaud, *Antivax*, p. 135.

Sacer,[299] in February 2020 began to negate the existence of the pandemic, presenting it as an instrumental pretense of bio-power to control the population. In an interview with *Le Monde* from March 24, 2020, he spoke of the existence of an "objective conspiracy" to impose a "state of exception,"[300] a term originating with the German legal theorist Carl Schmitt (1888–1985) that indicates the governing paradigm of modern society.[301]

The objective that governments pursued by means of the green pass, according to Agamben, is "the meticulous and unconditional control of every movement of its citizens, completely analogous to the internal passport that everyone in the Soviet Union had to carry to move from city to city."[302] His "state of exception" or "state of emergency" criticism was appreciated by right-libertarians. Libertarianism of the right, or anarcho-capitalism, supports the right to property and the free market, which the libertarianism of the left, or anarcho-communism, denies. Both the former and the latter propose the abolition of the state and of every form of social control, in the name of radical individualism.

In his book *Global Coup d 'Etat: Therapeutic Capitalism and the Great Reset*,[303] the Italian philosopher Diego Fusaro claims that we

[299] Giorgio Agamben, *Homo sacer. Il potere sovrano e la nuda vita* [*Homo Sacer: Sovereign Power and Bare Life*], Einaudi, Turin 1995.

[300] Agamben, "L'épidémie montre clairement que l'état d'exception est devenu la condition normale" [The epidemic clearly shows that a state of exception has become the norm], in *Le Monde*, March 24, 2020.

[301] Agamben, "Lo Stato di eccezione provocato da un'emergenza immotivata" [The State of Exception Provoked by an Unmotivated Emergency], in *Il Manifesto*, February 26, 2020.

[302] See Agamben, *A che punto siamo? L'epidemia come politica* [*Where Are We Now? The Epidemic as Politics*], and *Sul virus* [*On the Virus*], published by Quodlibet, Macerata 2020.

[303] Diego Fusaro, *Golpe globale. Capitalismo terapeutico e Grande Reset* [*Global Coup d 'Etat: Therapeutic Capitalism and the Great Reset*], Piemme, Milan 2021.

are witnessing a global coup, "on which the new techno-healthcare Leviathan of therapeutic capitalism has arisen"[304] to restructure society. Fusaro's philosophy of history is based on the lord–bondsman dialectic, a celebrated image from Hegel's *Phenomenology of Spirit*.[305] On the basis of Hegelian dialectic, Fusaro introduces a vertical juxtaposition between the Globalist Lord and the National Socialist Bondsman[306] and makes an appeal for a new political force which, assuming the point of view of the bondsman, works to construct what Gramsci defined as a new cultural and political hegemony. According to Fusaro, "this will have to be grounded in the re-verticalization of the conflict, such that the antagonism takes up once more an orientation in the 'bi-jective' form of the clash between bondsman and lord, between low and high, between base and apex," taking the structure "of the novel form of an ascensional rebellion against the plutocratic elites."[307]

The enemy is what the militant left-wing philosopher Antonio Negri defined by the term *empire*, in his work of the same name — the order of collective capital, in other words the force that won the civil war of the twentieth century,[308] a reality, for the anarcho-communists, that is not transitory, but absolute, limitless in space and eternal in time.

In the name of this anti-globalist and anti-elite rebellion, Fusaro, in his book *Think Otherwise*, exalts the great rebels of history against the constituted order: Prometheus, Spartacus, Luther, the

304 Ibid., p. 13.

305 G. W. F. Hegel, *Fenomenologia dello spirito* [*Phenomenology of Spirit*], ed. by Vincenzo Cicero, Rusconi, Milan 1995, pp. 275–89.

306 D. Fusaro, *Bentornato Gramsci. Undici tesi di filosofia della prassi* [*Welcome Back Gramsci: Eleven Theses of Philosophy of Practice*], La Nave di Teseo, Milan 2021, p. 353.

307 Ibid., p. 361.

308 Antonio Negri, *L'"Impero", stadio supremo dell'imperialismo* [*Empire, Final Phase of Imperialism*], in MD (I), January 2001, p. 3.

Anabaptists, Giordano Bruno, down to Marx, Lenin, Martin Luther King, Che Guevara and the anti-globalists.[309]

The new anti-globalist alliance coincides with *The Archipelago*, a work written by Massimo Cacciari that repudiates the state and every political and social order. In this he writes, "the space of the Archipelago is by its nature intolerant of subordination and hierarchical succession, no island constitutes the fixed axis capable of structuring the whole into the form of a state."[310]

Agamben too invites his readers to constitute a sort of clandestine network, a secret society: "dissidents need to think about creating something like a society within society, a community of friends and neighbors within the society of enmity and distance. The forms of this new clandestine existence that will have to become as autonomous as possible from institutions, will be from time to time considered and experimented, but only these will be able to guarantee human survival in a world which has decided on a more or less conscious self-destruction."[311]

How can we explain the participation in this global insurrection by the Archbishop Carlo Maria Viganò, according to whom "for the last two years we have been witnessing a global coup d'etat," before which "it is necessary to form an international anti-globalist alliance that gathers all those who seek to oppose the dictatorship, who do not intend to become slaves of a faceless power, who are not willing to cancel their own identity, their own individuality, their own religious faith. If the attack is global, the defense too must be global"?[312]

309 D. Fusaro, *Pensare altrimenti. Filosofia del dissenso* [*Think Otherwise: Philosophy of Dissent*], Einaudi, Turin 2017, pp. 3–4.

310 Massimo Cacciari, *L'Arcipelago* [*The Archipelago*], Adelphi, Milan 1997, p. 20.

311 Giorgio Agamben, "Una comunità nella società" [A Community Within Society], in *Quod Libet*. [https://www.quodlibet.it/giorgio-agamben-una-comunit-14-ella-societa].

312 Carlo Maria Viganò, *Appello per un'alleanza mondiale antiglobalista* [*Appeal for an Anti-Globalist World Alliance*], on November 18, 2021.

The new anti-globalism echoes the same themes of the anti-globalization movement that appeared on the media scene in Seattle, in December 1999, during a violent contestation of the World Trade Organization (WTO). The official birth of this movement of global insurrection occurred in the Brazilian city of Porto Alegre, on the occasion of the World Social Forum, held from January 25 to 30, 2001, to oppose the globalist WEF of Davos.

From the ideological baptism in Porto Alegre, it passed to that in Genoa on July 20, 2001, at which the anti-globalization movement showed the world its destructive power. "The declaration of war by the white suits," writes the extreme left-wing daily *The Manifesto*, "is a symbolic proclamation that gives a voice to an undeniable reality: the awaited challenger stepped onto the field, a 'movement of movements' ready to oppose openly the blind and arrogant greed of the powerful of the earth."[313] In a speech given on August 5, 2001, after the urban warfare of Genoa, Fidel Castro declared that it was a matter of "relighting the flame of the anti-imperialist struggle and of the progressive international forces after the terrible blow suffered ten years earlier with the end of the Soviet Union."[314]

Today, the inheritance of the anti-globalization movement of Seattle and Genoa has merged into a new anti-globalist movement with elusive borders, that moves in a virtual public square and has enlarged its spectrum of action from left to right. Within it coexist dialectically diverse ideological currents, from classical anarcho-insurrectionism to conservative anarcho-libertarianism, from neo-Gramscianism to some forms of neo-traditionalism, both Catholic and pagan.

What distinguishes this movement is its psychological disposition of radical pessimism and visceral refusal of power as such. Its

[313] Giuseppina Ciuffreda, "La sfida ai potenti della terra" [The Challenge to the Powerful of the Earth], in *Il Manifesto*, July 1, 2001.

[314] Massimo Caprara, "La via cubana per gli anti G8" [The Cuban Way for the Anti-G8], in *Il Giornale*, August 10, 2001.

destructive potential does not lie in violent manifestations, of which it is capable, but in a nihilistic ideology that accelerates the psychological and moral collapse of the West.

15. True Conspiracies and False Plots

To negate on principle the existence of secret forces that move history is as foolish and infantile as seeing plots everywhere without ever furnishing evidence of them.

Conspiracies and secret societies exist because man, wounded by original sin, is inclined to evil, and his social nature drives him to unite with others in realizing malicious objectives. When researching the existence of conspiracies throughout history one must shed light on their aims and means, and on their protagonists, to verify their reality. Nevertheless, Pope Leo XIII, in his letter *Custodi di quella fede,* defined Freemasonry as "a sect that after nineteen centuries of Christian civilization endeavors to destroy the Catholic Church." He warned that one need not "exaggerate the power of Freemasonry, attributing to her direct and immediate action all the evils which, in the religious order, presently afflict us."[315]

Conspiracies, like *congiure,* are real if they have definite protagonists and if they are situated in time and in a circumscribed place. The fictitious plot, on the other hand, is an evasive and occult aggregate, of which the identity of the protagonists is not revealed, nor is the concrete operative modality. The theory that spread in Catholic circles of the macro-epidemiological plot appears vague and confused, lacking consequent logical passages and an adequate document base.

There is often a chain of interactions among conspiracies that occur in diverse times and places. But the theorists of macro-plots

[315] Leone XIII, Lettera *Custodi di quella fede* [*Custodians of the Faith*] of December 8, 1892, Acta, vol. XII (1893), p. 337 and pp. 334–35 (pp. 331–43).

cite a variety of names and events without demonstrating their connections, often basing their assumptions on the sophism "*Post hoc, ergo propter hoc*" (This happened after that, therefore that is the cause of this), for which one presumes a causal relationship between the two circumstances, due to the simple fact that one occurs after the other. The sophism lies in substituting the causal link that ought to characterize every operation of our reasoning process with a purely temporal connection, supposing that if one event follows another, the first must be the cause of the second. In reality, a temporal succession is necessary that there be a causal relation, given that every effect must be preceded by a cause, but this temporal link is not sufficient to demonstrate anything. The chronological order does not necessarily coincide with the logical order.

The existence of secret forces implies the existence of hidden projects. This does not mean that everything that happens is planned and that all projects necessarily translate into reality. History does not follow an obligatory course, and can also change due to unexpected and unpredictable events. The principle of causality, which holds the universe in being, belongs to the metaphysical and not to the mechanical order, and allows for the existence of "chance" and things that are imponderable for those who live in history, but not for God who transcends and guides it.

Stefan Zweig (1881–1942) dedicated a book to what he defined as the "fatal moments," those "in which the scales of history are suspended in equilibrium."[316] For the Austrian writer, human destiny depends on that ephemeral weave of destiny that the Greeks called *kairòs*. Those like Zweig who lack a supernatural vision of history attribute to destiny, or to chance, the events that, without an apparent logic, determine unexpected historical shifts; those who are inspired by a

316 Stefan Zweig, *Momenti fatali* [*Fatal Moments*], tr. It., Adelphi, Milan 2005 (1927).

Christian theology of history know that chance does not exist, but that all that happens is foreseen and regulated by God, including the realization or failure of the designs of secret forces.

St. Thomas Aquinas explains this. That which is fortuitous or chance-like with respect to an inferior cause, insofar as it occurs outside of its intention, is not fortuitous or properly chance with respect to a superior cause, insofar as it is not produced outside of its intention: "This is evident, for example, in the case of the master who sends two servants to the same place, though they do not know they are both going there. Their meeting is chance for both of them, but not for the master who sent them."[317] Not all conspiracies succeed, because there exist unintended outcomes, or to borrow a term from the sociologist Jules Monnerot (1908–1995), there is *heterotely*, which interposes between the project and its fulfillment.[318]

The plotting spirit denies chance and the imponderable, attributing not to God, but to human agents, the unforeseeable factors of history. The plotting spirit presumes to render the mystery rational, but substitutes logical reasoning with "analogical" reasoning, typical of esoterism, according to which there exist invisible relations between all levels of reality throughout the universe, which would be "a sort of hall of mirrors pervaded and animated by invisible forces."[319] To this refusal of logic there corresponds a refusal of the order of being, based on the inversion of roles between reason and imagination and the choice to renounce the experience of what one has imagined.

The principle *cui prodest* or *cui bono* (who benefits from a certain event) can constitute the basis for an investigative hypothesis, but as

[317] Aquinas, *Compendio di teologia* [*Summa Teologia*] Edizioni Studio Domenicano, Bologna 1995, p. 169.

[318] Jules Monnerot, *L'intelligence de la politique* [*The Intelligence of Politics*], Gauthier-Villars, Paris 1977, pp. 3 ff.

[319] Antoine Faivre, *L'esoterismo occidentale. Metodi, temi, immagini* [*Western Esoterism: Methods, Themes, Images*] tr. It. Morcelliana, Brescia 2012, p. 17.

such it does not determine anything: it must be proved by facts that transform the evidence into demonstration. To say, for example, that because the pharmaceutical companies enriched themselves during the pandemic, they are the cause of epidemics, would be like affirming that because the makers of bombs draw economic advantages from wars, bomb manufacturers are the cause of wars. This might be true within an economistic perspective, but it is certainly inadmissible in a Christian conception of history.

In the case of the coronavirus pandemic, while holding that public opinion was manipulated by mass media and suffered a sort of societal hypnosis, it seems difficult to believe, without any evidence, that the totality of scientists and doctors around the world, as well as all heads of states and governments, could have shared the secret of the inexistence of the pandemic and of the reality of the conspiracy and associated to carry it out. This would make it the first democratic conspiracy in history, with the participation of hundreds of thousands of conspirators, which would contradict the idea of a plot hatched by a tight group of elite masters of the world.

Everything is possible in history, but to distinguish the possible from the real one needs to remember that the truth is "the mind's conformity to how things are."[320] The plotting spirit overturns the traditional principle for which what is real is true, and affirms that the virus does not exist because it is not "true," and that the conspiracy is true because it exists. This form of knowledge, based on the short circuit of thought, is typical of Gnosis, according to which the truth of an intellectual system does not lie in its adherence to an objective truth, but in its capacity to self-justify: "The system is justified by the fact of being constructed; the possibility of raising objections about the construction of systems as such is not allowed."[321]

[320] Aquinas, *Summa theologiae*, I, q. 17, a. 4.

[321] E. Voegelin, *Il mito del mondo nuovo* [*The Myth of the New World*], p. 112.

The declared enemy of the anti-globalists is the "system" as such. However, wherever a society exists, there exists an establishment that unites an elite of rulers who, in a more or less legitimate manner, holds power. The criticism of the plotting spirit seems to focus upon not the arbitrary use of power, but upon power as such, a "power without a face," of which the plot constitutes the essence. "The idea behind this," observes Donatella Di Cesare, "is that the world has become a conspiracy and the conspiracy has become a world."[322]

This position corresponds to that of the Gnostics, whose anti-cosmism is born of their hatred for the world, created in their view by the "bad god" of the Old Testament. The aim of Gnosticism has always been that of "undoing" creation by means of a plan of global chaos, founded on the destruction of every logical and metaphysical determination of reality. The Gospel of Judas, according to which Jesus is at war with the evil creator of this world, is one of the fundamental texts of this new Gnosis.[323] In this pseudo-Gospel, which is in reality a Jewish Gnostic text, Judas is presented as the most elevated of Christ's followers, the only one to whom Jesus entrusted the secret wisdom necessary for salvation. This corresponds to what St. Irenaeus writes about the Cainites: for them, "the traitor Judas, alone among all those knowing the truth, fulfilled the mystery of betrayal."[324]

The existence of a vast convergence of forces and interests to demolish the religious, moral, and civic principles upon which Christian civilization has stood for centuries is before the eyes of all. "Who can ignore," admonished Leo XIII over a century ago, "how

[322] Donatella Di Cesare, *Il complotto al potere* [*Conspiracy in Power*], Einaudi, Turin 2021, pp. 23–24.

[323] *Vangelo di Giuda. Estratto dal Codex Tchacos* [*The Gospel of Judas: Extract from the Tchacos Codex*], ed. by Rodolphe Kasser, Marvin Meyer, Gregor Wurst, National Geographic Society - White Star, Vercelli 2006.

[324] St. Irenaeus, *Contro le eresie* [*Against Heresies*], tr. It. Cantagalli, Siena 1968, vol. I, p. 14.

large is the conspiracy of forces which today aims at upending and dispersing the great work of Jesus Christ, attempting with an obstinacy that knows no bounds, to destroy on the intellectual plane, the treasure of heavenly doctrine, to subvert on the social plane the most holy, most wholesome Christian institutions?"[325]

The revolutionary forces, obvious or hidden, have attempted in vain to construct a modern civilization antithetical to Christian civilization. All their efforts have failed, and a plan of global destruction has replaced the dream of a New World Order, which constitutes the essence of the Revolution. "The final aim of Freemasonry," as the final document of the anti-Masonic conference in Trent established, "is the universal destruction of the physical, intellectual, and moral order by means of the principle '*per peccatum mors.*' "[326]

Among the Gnostic prophets of our time is Dom Léger-Marie Deschamps (1716–1774), a Benedictine monk and an atheist, who secretly influenced Diderot and the French encyclopedists. His manuscripts were rediscovered nearly a century after his death and published for the first time in Bolshevik Russia, in 1930. Igor Safarevic[327] and Bronislaw Baczko (1924–2016)[328] highlighted the significance of these writings in which Deschamps proclaims general equality as a universal law: "All beings flow out and flow into one another and all are nothing but diverse aspects of one universal kind."[329]

325 Leo XIII, Apostolic Letter *Annum ingressi*, p. 1895.

326 *Actes du 1er Congrès Antimaçonnique international* [*Acts of the First International Anti-Masonic Conference*], cit., p. 36.

327 I. Safarevic, *Il socialismo come fenomeno storico mondiale* [*Socialism as a Global Historical Phenomenon*], cit., pp. 108–60.

328 Bronislaw Baczko, *L'utopia. Immaginazione sociale e rappresentazioni utopiche nell'età dell'illuminismo* [*Utopia: Social Imagination and Utopian Representations in the Enlightenment Age*], tr. It. Einaudi, Turin 1979, pp. 102–56.

329 I. Safarevic, *Il socialismo come fenomeno storico mondiale* [*Socialism as a Global Historical Phenomenon*], p. 144.

Pantheism coincides with nihilism because all is nothing and all must become nothing. The radical post-Enlightenment doctrines of Theosophy, Nazism, and Communism reveal to us that the true face of revolution that has assaulted Christian civilization for seven centuries is the dream of an integral metaphysical and social disorder. It is no wonder to learn from the master of the Kabbalah Gershom Scholem that the Marxist philosopher György Lukács (1885–1971) confided to the revolutionary journalist Ilona Duczynska (1897–1978) that "nihilism was the secret doctrine of Communism."[330]

Gnostic cosmogony, found throughout the esoteric doctrines that run down the centuries, penetrates even the Catholic Church and permeates the mentality of neo-modernism, but also that of the new plotting movements that have nothing to do with the study of secret, antichristian societies, which have always been part of historiography and of Catholic apologetics. This vague and confused new plotting movement plays into the hands of those who seek to destabilize the West psychologically, intellectually, and morally.

The false cosmogonies have always been disseminated by revolutionary agents to invalidate the true criticism of that antichristian revolution that is inspired by the devil, described by St. Paul as "the god of this world" (2 Cor. 4:4) and "prince of the power of the air" (Eph. 2:2). We cannot comprehend history without reference to God, first cause and final end of all that moves in the universe. But neither can we ignore the existence of Satan, who uses in history the power that God accords him to draw out of evil the maximum good for His glory.

The current confusion constitutes just one more proof of the existence of the devil. The lugubrious laugh of the prince of darkness, theorist of every true conspiracy and author of every false plot,

[330] G. Scholem, *Le tre vite di Moses Dobrushka* [*The Three Lives of Moses Dobrushka*], pp. 212–13.

does not frighten those who trust in God, whose Providence protects and governs all He has created. In fact, this Providence "reaches mightily from one end of the earth to the other, and she orders all things well" (Wis. 8:1). The devil is incapable of making history, and incapable of undoing it as he would like. It is God, and He alone, who guides history supernaturally for His glory and for the sanctification of the elect. It is around the saints, and not around evil, that the world turns, as St. Paul affirms when he says, "*Omnia sustineo propter electos*" (I endure everything for the sake of the elect," 2 Tim. 2:10). To follow the path of the saints is the only way to avoid losing oneself in the pathways of evil.

About the Author

Roberto de Mattei is a historian who has taught at the University of Rome, "La Sapienza," the University of Cassino, and the European University of Rome. From 2003 to 2011, he served two terms as vice president of the National Research Council of Italy. He is the president of the Lepanto Foundation and the director of the periodical *Radici Cristiane* and of the information agency Corrispondenza Romana. He has collaborated with numerous newspapers and periodicals, such as *L'Osservatore Romano*, *Libero*, *Il Giornale d'Italia*, *Il Tempo*, and *Il Foglio*, and is the author of more than thirty books translated into multiple languages, among which are *The Second Vatican Council: A History Never Written*, which received the Acqui-Storia Prize in 2011; *The Rally of Leo XIII: The Failure of a Pastoral Project*; *Criticism of Revolution in the Thought of Augusto Del Noce*; *Pius V: The History of a Holy Pope*; *Turkey in Europe: Beneficial or Catastrophe?*; and *The Church in the Tempest*, taken from conversations broadcast on Radio Maria.

Sophia Institute

SOPHIA INSTITUTE IS A nonprofit institution that seeks to nurture the spiritual, moral, and cultural life of souls and to spread the gospel of Christ in conformity with the authentic teachings of the Roman Catholic Church.

Sophia Institute Press fulfills this mission by offering translations, reprints, and new publications that afford readers a rich source of the enduring wisdom of mankind.

Sophia Institute also operates the popular online resource CatholicExchange.com. *Catholic Exchange* provides world news from a Catholic perspective as well as daily devotionals and articles that will help readers to grow in holiness and live a life consistent with the teachings of the Church.

In 2013, Sophia Institute launched Sophia Institute for Teachers to renew and rebuild Catholic culture through service to Catholic education. With the goal of nurturing the spiritual, moral, and cultural life of souls, and an abiding respect for the role and work of teachers, we strive to provide materials and programs that are at once enlightening to the mind and ennobling to the heart; faithful and complete, as well as useful and practical.

Sophia Institute gratefully recognizes the Solidarity Association for preserving and encouraging the growth of our apostolate over the course of many years. Without their generous and timely support, this book would not be in your hands.

www.SophiaInstitute.com
www.CatholicExchange.com
www.SophiaInstituteforTeachers.org

Sophia Institute Press is a registered trademark of Sophia Institute.
Sophia Institute is a tax-exempt institution as defined by the
Internal Revenue Code, Section 501(c)(3). Tax ID 22-2548708.